Literary Criticism and Cultural Theory

Edited by

William E. Cain
Professor of English
Wellesley College

A Routledge Series

Literary Criticism and Cultural Theory

William E. Cain, *General Editor*

Contested Masculinities
Crises in Colonial Male Identity from Joseph Conrad to Satyajit Ray
Nalin Jayasena

Unsettled Narratives
The Pacific Writings of Stevenson, Ellis, Melville and London
David Farrier

The Subject of Race in American Science Fiction
Sharon DeGraw

Parsing the City
Jonson, Middleton, Dekker, and City Comedy's London as Language
Heather C. Easterling

The Economy of the Short Story in British Periodicals of the 1890s
Winnie Chan

Negotiating the Modern
Orientalism and Indianness in the Anglophone World
Amit Ray

Novels, Maps, Modernity
The Spatial Imagination, 1850–2000
Eric Bulson

Novel Notions
Medical Discourse and the Mapping of the Imagination in Eighteenth-Century English Fiction
Katherine E. Kickel

Masculinity and the English Working Class
Studies in Victorian Autobiography and Fiction
Ying S. Lee

Aesthetic Hysteria
The Great Neurosis in Victorian Melodrama and Contemporary Fiction
Ankhi Mukherjee

The Rise of Corporate Publishing and Its Effects on Authorship in Early Twentieth-Century America
Kim Becnel

Conspiracy, Revolution, and Terrorism from Victorian Fiction to the Modern Novel
Adrian S. Wisnicki

City/Stage/Globe
Performance and Space in Shakespeare's London
D.J. Hopkins

Transatlantic Engagements with the British Eighteenth Century
Pamela Albert

Race, Immigration, and American Identity in the Fiction of Salman Rushdie, Ralph Ellison, and William Faulkner
Randy Boyagoda

Cosmopolitan Culture and Consumerism in Chick Lit
Caroline J. Smith

Asian Diaspora Poetry in North America
Benzi Zhang

Asian Diaspora Poetry in North America

Benzi Zhang

New York London

First published 2008
by Routledge
711 Third Avenue, New York, NY 10017

Simultaneously published in the UK
by Routledge
2 Park Square, Milton Park, Abingdon, Oxon OX14 4RN

Routledge is an imprint of the Taylor & Francis Group, an informa business

First issued in paperback 2011

Typeset in Adobe Garamond by IBT Global

Library of Congress Cataloging in Publication Data
Zhang, Benzi.
Asian diaspora poetry in North America / by Benzi Zhang.
p. cm.— (Literary criticism and cultural theory)
Includes bibliographical references and index.
ISBN-13: 978-0-415-95717-5 (acid-free paper)
ISBN-10: 0-415-95717-6 (acid-free paper) 1. American poetry--Asian American authors--History and criticism. 2. Canadian poetry--Asian authors--History and criticism. 3. Asian diaspora. 4. Asian Americans--Ethnic identity. 5. Group identity in literature. 6. Multiculturalism in literature. 7. Memory in literature. 8. Other (Philosophy) in literature. I. Title.

PS153.A84Z63 2007
810.9'895--dc22 2007021230

ISBN13: 978-0-415-95717-5 (hbk)
ISBN13: 978-0-203-93724-2 (ebk)
ISBN13: 978-0-415-51286-2 (pbk)

To Yuwei

Unfettered at last, a traveling monk,
I pass the old Zen barrier.
Mine is a traceless stream-and-cloud life.
Of those mountains, which shall be my home?

Manan, *The Penguin Book of Zen Poetry* (1997, 76)

Every thinking that is on the trail of something is a poetizing, and all poetry a thinking.

Martin Heidegger, *Basic Writings* (1993, 425)

Contents

Contents

Acknowledgments

The process of writing this book is diasporic. It connected me to many discursive and non-discursive locations and built me relationships with numerous people. At this moment, I would like to acknowledge the support, inspiration and encouragement that I have received from a transnational community of friends, colleagues, authors and co-diasporas. My deep gratitude goes to Robert Wilson and Robin Cohen for their encouragement. I benefited from edifying conversations with Wing Tek Lum on poetic imagination. I am indebted to George Perkins for his feedback on earlier versions of the manuscript and to James Phelan for his help with research. I am grateful to William E. Cain and Max Novick for their support of this project. I also owe a special note of thanks to Nurjehan Aziz, Mei-Mei Berssenbrugge, Diana Chang, Ha Jin, Joy Kogawa, Russell Leong, Walter K. Lew, Shirley Geok-lin Lim, Roy Miki, David Mura, Cathy Song, M. G. Vassanji, Fred Wah, Jeannie L. Wong, Nellie Wong, Jim Wong-Chu, John Yau and Cyn. Zarco. The research assistance provided by Daphne Kang, Priscilla Ng and Flora Yip is deeply appreciated.

Parts of the work have appeared in print before. Special acknowledgment is due to the editors of *Journal of American Studies, College Literature* and *Journal of Intercultural Studies*. In particular, I want to express my gratitude to S. Jay Kleinberg, Susan Castillo, Kostas Myrsiades and Georgina Tsolidis. I would also like to thank the professional associations whose conferences gave me the opportunities to present portions of the study to various kinds of audience. I received useful comments from participants at American Literature Association Conference (Cambridge, Massachusetts), the Conference of the Society for the Study of Multi-ethnic Literatures of the United States (Boca Raton, Florida), American Comparative Literature Association Conference (New Haven, Connecticut), the Convention of Midwest Modern Language Association (Cleveland, Ohio), and the Conference of Canadian Association for Commonwealth Literature and Language Studies (London, Canada). Finally, I wish to acknowledge the generous support from the Research Grants Council of HKSAR, which provides the grant needed to complete the project.

B. Z.

Acknowledgements

Permissions

Past" and "To Ah Shu" by permission of Hanging Loose Press. Copyright © 1996 by Ha Jin. Excerpt from "To an Ancient Chinese Poet" by permission of the poet. Copyright © 1990 by Ha Jin. Jessica Hagedorn: Excerpts from "Autobiography Part One" and "Souvenirs" by permission of City Lights Books. Copyright © 2002 by Jessica Hagedorn. Kimiko Hahn: Excerpt from "The Izu Dancer" by permission of Hanging Loose Press. Copyright © 1992 by Kimiko Hahn. Garrett Hongo: Excerpts from "O-Bon: Dance for the Dead" and "The Legend" by permission of Random House. Copyright © 1996 by Garrett Hongo. Lawson Fusao Inada: Excerpts from "In a Buddhist Forest" and "Kicking the Habit" by permission of Coffee House Press. Copyright © 1997 by Lawson Fusao Inada. Excerpts from "Memory," "Headwaters" and "Red Earth, Blue Sky, Petrified" by permission of Coffee House Press. Copyright © 1993 by Lawson Fusao Inada. Kevin Irie: Excerpt from "Flight: An Immigrant's Memory" by permission of TSAR. Copyright © 1996 by Kevin Irie. Jam Ismail: Excerpt from "From Scared Texts" by permission of Douglas and McIntyre. Copyright © 1991 by Jam Ismail. Sally Ito: "Sansei" by permission of the poet. Copyright © 1996 by Sally Ito. Surjeet Kalsey: Excerpts from "Breaking the Silence" and "Migratory Birds" by permission of TSAR. Copyright © 1990 by Surjeet Kalsey. Myung Mi Kim: Excerpt from "Anna O Addendum" by permission of the poet. Copyright © 1995 by Myung Mi Kim. Joy Kogawa: Excerpts from "She is not a Fence Sitter," "For Ben and Malcolm" and "Minerals from Stone" by permission of the poet. Copyright © 1985 by Joy Kogawa. Excerpt from "Once When We Were Rejected" by permission of McClelland and Stewart. Copyright © 1977 by Joy Kogawa. Excerpt from "This is a Clearing" by permission of the poet. Copyright © 1974 by Joy Kogawa. Lydia Kwa: Excerpt from "Travelling Time" by permission of the poet. Copyright © 1994 by Lydia Kwa. Laiwan: "The Imperialism of Syntax" by permission of Douglas and McIntyre. Copyright © 1991 by Laiwan. Christian Langworthy: Excerpt from "How I Could Interpret the Events of my Youth, Events I do not Remember except in Dreams" by permission of the poet. Copyright © 2000 by Christian Langworthy. Evelyn Lau: "The Monks' Song" by permission of the poet. Copyright © 1994 by Evelyn Lau. Li-Young Lee: Excerpts from "Discrepancies, Happy and Sad" and "Restless" by permission of BOA Editions. Copyright © 2001 by Li-Young Lee. Excerpt from "Furious Versions" by permission of BOA Editions. Copyright © 1990 by Li-Young Lee. Excerpts from "The Gift" and "Mnemonic" by permission of BOA Editions. Copyright © 1986 by Li-Young Lee. Pwu Jean Lee: "A Guitar" by permission of the poet. Copyright © 1997 by Pwu Jean Lee. Russell Leong: Excerpts from "Aerogrammes" and "Flume" by permission of West End Press. Copyright © 1993 by Russell Leong. Ho Hon Leung: Excerpt from "A Symphonic Poem 'Unfinished'" by permission of the poet. Copyright © 1983 by Ho Hon Leung. Shirley Geok-lin Lim: Excerpt from "Father in China" by permission of the poet. Copyright © 1999 by Shirley Geok-lin Lim. Excerpts from "I Remember," "To What Ends," "An Immigrant Looks at Whitman" and "I Defy You" by permission of the poet. Copyright © 1994 by Shirley Geok-lin Lim. Stephen Liu: "My Father's Martial Art" by permission of the Antioch Review, Inc. Copyright © 1981 by the Antioch Review, Inc. Timothy Liu: Excerpt from "Awaiting Translation" by permission of Alice James Books. Copyright © 1992 by Timothy Liu. Wing Tek Lum: "Chinese Hot Pot" and "T-Bone Steak" by permission of the poet. Copyright © 1991 by Wing Tek Lum. Manan: "Unfettered at last, a traveling monk" by permission of Grave/Atlantic, Inc. Copyright © 1997 by Lucien Stryk. Diane Mei Lin Mark: "Suzie Wong Doesn't Live Here" by permission of the poet. Copyright © 1991 by Diane Mei Lin Mark. Roy Miki: Excerpt from "Market Rinse" by permission of the poet. Copyright © 1995 by Roy Miki. David Mura: "Issei: Song of the First Years in America" by permission of the poet. Copyright © 1995 by David Mura. Lucy Ng: Excerpts from "The Sullen Shapes of Poems" by permission of Douglas and McIntyre. Copyright © 1991 by Lucy Ng. Uma Parameswaran: "Sharad" by permission of the poet. Copyright © 1990 by Uma Parameswaran. Saleem Peeradina: "Reflections on the Other" by permission of Westview Press. Copyright © 1995 by Saleem Peeradina. Tilottama Rajan: Excerpt from "Victims of the War" by permission of TSAR. Copyright © 1990 by Tilottama Rajan. Thelma Seto: "Living in the Margins" by permission of the poet. Copyright © 1995 by Thelma Seto. Cathy Song: Excerpt from "Heaven" by permission of the poet. Copyright © 1988 by Cathy Song. Excerpt from "Beauty and Sadness" by permission of Yale University Press. Copyright © 1983 by Cathy Song. Ben Soo: Excerpt from "Prentiss and the Island" by permission of Douglas and McIntyre. Copyright © 1991 by Ben Soo. Arthur Sze: Excerpts from "The Network" and "Every Where and Every When" by permission of Copper Canyon Press. Copyright © 1998 by Arthur Sze. Excerpt from "Archipelago" by permission of Copper Canyon Press. Copyright © 1995 by Arthur Sze. Lê Thi Diem Thúy: Excerpt from "Shrapnel Shards on Blue Water" by permission of the poet and Aragi, Inc. First published in Water Magazine. Copyright © 2000 by Lê Thi Diem Thúy. Jora Trang: "Legacy" by permission of the poet. Copyright © 2000 by Jora Trang. Amita Vasudeva: "Can you Talk Mexican?" by permission of Westview Press. Copyright © 1995 by Amita Vasudeva. Thuong Vuong-Riddick, "Searching," "Day and Night" and "For My Father" by permission of Ronsdale Press. Copyright © 1995 by Thuong Vuong-Riddick. Fred Wah:

Excerpts from "Elite" by permission of Douglas and McIntyre. Copyright © 1995 by Fred Wah. Excerpts from "mmmmmm," "WHAT'S IT LIKE TO HOLD YOURSELF IN" and "WANT RIVER PIECE OUT OF THIS MOVING RIVER" by permission of the poet. Copyright © 1981 by Fred Wah. Excerpt from "Pictograms from the Interior of B.C." by permission of the poet. Copyright © 1980 by Fred Wah. Nellie Wong: Excerpt from "It's in the Blood" by permission of the poet. Copyright © 2003 by Nellie Wong. Rita Wong: "grammar poem" by permission of the poet. Copyright © 1999 by Rita Wong. Jim Wong-Chu: "How Feel I Do?" by permission of the poet. Copyright © 1991 by Jim Wong-Chu. "Peasants," "Fourth Uncle" and "Old Chinese Cemetery: Kamloops July 1977" by permission of the poet. Copyright © 1996 by Jim Wong-Chu. "Tradition" by permission of the poet. Copyright © 1986 by Jim Wong-Chu. David Woo: "Habit" by permission of the poet. Copyright © 1993 by David Woo. Merle Woo: Excerpt from "Yellow Woman Speaks" by permission of the poet. Copyright © 1991 by Merle Woo. Mitsuye Yamada: Excerpt from "Block 4 Barrack 4 'Apt' C." by permission of the poet. Copyright © 1991 by Mitsuye Yamada. Excerpts from "Desert Run" and "Masks of Woman" by permission of the poet. Copyright © 1988 by Mitsuye Yamada. John Yau: "830 Fireplace Road" by permission of the poet. Copyright © 2002 by John Yau. "Genghis Chan: Private Eye XXV" and "Genghis Chan: Private Eye XXVII" by permission of the poet. Copyright © 1996 by John Yau. "Postcard 16" by permission of the poet. Copyright © 1992 by John Yau. Cyn. Zarco: "Magdalena's Vision" by permission of the poet. Copyright © 1995 by Cyn. Zarco. Zhen Zhang:"Deep into Småland" by permission of the poet. Copyright © 1999 by Zhen Zhang.

Chapter One

Introduction

Departure for a Detour

How does *distancing* produce an effect? Westerners find it natural and normal to meet the world head-on. But what can we gain from approaching it *obliquely*? In other words, how does detour grant access?

François Jullien

Detour and Access (2000, 7)

The notion of diaspora has been deployed both literally and figuratively to designate a particular opportunity for reinvention and liberation from various naturalized categories, set within historical contingencies that weigh into the production of such subjectivities.

David Palumbo-Liu

Asian/American (1999, 343)

Asian diaspora poetry in North America is a rich body of poetic works which, on the one hand, provides valuable materials for us to understand the lives and experiences of Asian diasporas and, on the other, offers us an opportunity to examine some of the most important issues in current literary and cultural studies. As a mode of writing across cultural and national borders, these poetic works challenge us to reconsider the assumptions and meanings of identity, nation, home, place and memory in a broad cross-cultural context. In recent critical inquiries, diaspora has been conceived not only as a process of migration in which people crossed and traversed the borders of different countries, but also as a double relationship between different cultural homes/origins. The reconceptualization of diaspora as a relationship, according to Smadar Lavie and Ted Swedenburg, enables us to "understand the dynamics of transnational cultural and economic processes, as well as to challenge the conceptual limits imposed by national and ethnic/racial boundaries" (1996, 14). With all its complexity and ambiguity associated with the experience of multicultural mediation, diaspora, as both a process and a relationship, suggests an act of constant repositioning in confluent streams that accommodate multiple cultural traditions. By examining how Asian diaspora poets maintain and represent their cultural differences in North America, we will seek new perspectives for understanding and analyzing the development of Asian cultural heritages that survive persistently and change constantly in American and Canadian societies. This book, therefore, will offer a fresh point of departure for our exploration of how Asian diaspora poetry plays a significant role in mediating and defining cross-cultural and transnational positions.

For many years, criticism of Asian diaspora poetry has mainly worked within the boundaries of Asian American literary and ethnic studies. In the age of globalization and postcolonialism, however, the significance of Asian diaspora writings has actually gone far beyond the traditional boundaries; and the reading of Asian diaspora poetry, as a result, demands new approaches that would expand the field of ethnic literatures by embracing cross-cultural, transnational and postcolonial inquiries. Probably as a response to the increasing involvement of transnational and cross-cultural interactions in the age of globalization, a "significant switch in emphasis has also occurred in Asian American literary studies," as King-kok Cheung observes; "the stress is now on heterogeneity and diaspora" and "the shift has been from seeking to 'claim America' to forging a connection between Asia and Asian America" (1997, 1). By exploring the cross-cultural connections between Asia and America, this study will examine how Asian diaspora poetry has developed itself in a process of negotiating across different cultural traditions in a global context. "The massive social, cultural, and political dislocations and realignments characterizing the end of the twentieth century," according to Sunn Shelley Wong, "call for new strategic namings, new 'words' to enable us to see into the conditions of our own time and place and to clear the ground for future possibilities" (2001, 302). Since Asian diaspora poetry inscribes an international mode of thinking and a way of living between cultures, a diasporic perspective is needed in the reading of those exceptional poetic works whose relations to Asia and to other parts of the world are much more complex and extensive than we have imagined. It is important to go beyond the limits of ethnic and national approaches in the study of Asian diaspora poetry, for cross-cultural and inter-national investigations will produce a better understanding of diasporic identity and writing whose structures and perimeters do not coincide with the borders of singular nation-states. As Robin Cohen asserts, it is no longer necessary "to imprison the butterfly of ethnic identity in too small a net with too dense a mesh. Perhaps the butterfly should be permitted to fly in its own direction at its own whim" (1997, 126).

Diaspora, as Shirley Lim put it, "denotes a condition of being deprived of the affiliation of nation, not temporally situated on its way toward another totality, but fragmented, demonstrating provisionality and exigency as immediate, unmediated presence. The discourse of diaspora is that of disarticulation of identity from natal and national resources, and includes the exilic imagination but is not restricted to it" (1997, 297). In our discussion, the idea of diaspora suggests a shift from national to inter-national and cross-cultural contextualizations. Traditionally, the study of literature is charted in national categories. In the age of globalization and postcolonialism, however, the situation has changed, as diasporic paradigm becomes increasingly important for comparative analyses of the ideological and cultural imaginaries among what has been considered as discrete national groups. The shift to "the discourse of diaspora," in Lim's words, "is one example of the dynamics of an evolving global technology capable of transmitting information simultaneously through mass media to geographically separate yet culturally related peoples" (1997, 297). Asian diasporas, as a result, should not be "seen as bound to a context exclusively that of their host country," as Franklin Ng contends; "Instead, the immigrants and their descendents are seen as part of a global phenomenon of international migration and cultural diasporas" (1998, ix).

The strategic naming of Asian diaspora is not simply designated as an ethnic descriptor; but rather it suggests a theoretical detour towards new vantage points with emphasis on the practice of diaspora theory whereby various models of inquiries are set into play outside the confines of singular nation-states. In both figural and practical senses, detours provide a way of transcending the limitations of our perception and breaking the obstructions of our thought. According to François Jullien, only through detours can we create a new space for thinking from a distant standpoint and move out of the self-enclosure of subjectivity. For that reason, we will follow a detour between Asia and North America to explore how the symbolic power of cultural forces has been poetized across geographic and historical divides. The paradox of detour is that by traveling to "Asia," we may get access to a better understanding of "America" or vice versa. "I expect that this detour through China," in Jullien's words, "will open up a perspective: the ability to question ourselves from the outside" (2000, 371). If going outside is a necessary procedure for gaining insight, the study of Asian diaspora poetry would be a multifold journey of interrogative detours at different levels, which will lead us to grasp and to have a dialogue with a number of intricate issues that cannot be perceived or accounted for otherwise. This book, therefore, is not a direct survey of Asian diaspora poetry, but rather an oblique exploration of some major aspects of the poetic works in a vast labyrinth of diaspora.

"Diaspora always takes place after a border crossing," as David Palumbo-Liu observes (1999, 346). In my discussion, however, border-crossing is figured as a complex multifold process. Asian diaspora poetry concerns not only the movement across the borders of a country, but also the experiences of traversing the boundaries and barriers of space, time, race, culture, language and history. Since diaspora develops multiple relationships that cross and span cultural and national borders, it shifts our attention away from a narrow focus on ethnic relations at the local level to a broad concern with transnational relationships in a large system of global signification. In the following chapter, "the Poetics of Cultural Transrelation," we will examine how Asian diaspora poetry disrupts the apparent closure of nationality and generates transnational communications. With its ethnic vacillation and cultural ambivalence, Asian diaspora poetry demonstrates that the forces of different national elements may merge in a poetics of cultural transrelation, which challenges the locality of a singular cultural dominance by relocating the site of identity formation in a collective of plural interrelationships. Cultural transrelation, therefore, seeks to compare and to connect different cultural and national elements in the articulation of new identities. In this sense, cultural transrelation does not mean to find equivalence in different cultures for substitution, but to expand the space of continuity in which various cultural traditions are negotiated and reconfigured into new viable forms. Moreover, cultural transrelation indicates a phenomenon of cultural defamiliarization in which one may see one's own past and culture as foreign otherness. This paradoxical transposition between two cultural frames causes Asian diaspora poets to re-view their historical experiences and cultural inheritances in a new context and to interpret them from a fresh perspective.

Cultural transrelation is informed as well as complicated by the issue of multi-home conditions. In the chapter entitled "the Politics of Re-homing," we will argue that the earlier conceptualizations of home based on a singular location are no longer adequate to describe the new dimensions and transformations of home. In a sense, Asian diaspora poetry represents a paradoxical feeling of both homesickness and home-crisis, for the movement between multiple locations of cultures suggests a cobelonging dialogue which, by situating diasporas simultaneously inside and outside of a culture, intensifies both the desirability and the impossibility of a given home-place. Adrift between two or more different sociocultural systems that cannot be fully integrated, Asian diasporas are subject to a constant rehoming process in which various elements of foreignness and otherness are reconfigured and repositioned in relation to new cultural dwellings and indwellings. In modern diaspora, therefore, to rehome is not to go home but to undergo a constructive process in which different cultural passages are convoluted to produce new senses of dwelling around the "axis of a mobility." Rehoming, furthermore, carries special meanings for women diaspora poets, whose writings often present a strong voice in their strife to challenge the hegemonic, totalizing discourse of male-dominated ideology of home. Re-versing home in their own ways, they develop a critical consciousness in diasporic discourse and adopt new approaches that embrace female consciousness, questioning rather than celebrating the patriarchal values of traditional home.

The rehoming process, furthermore, has touched a sensitive nerve of the global system in which the concept of place has to be reconsidered. In the chapter on "the Problematics of Translocal Place," we will make a few inquiries into Asian diaspora poetry with emphasis on the relationship between the changing meaning of place and the articulation of diasporic identity. As mutual penetration among different cultural locations has dramatically increased, we need to explore the influence as well as the consequence of place-in-displacement on the formation of identity across cultural and national boundaries. In the age of modern diaspora, it is almost impossible to segregate any local place that does not involve nonlocal or extralocal linkages in a wide network. What Asian diaspora poetry represents is a dramatic change in the politics of place, which starts to redefine place beyond the historical opposition of *here* versus *there*, since to a certain extent, *there* has been both merged and emerged in the very characterization of *here*. "It is a sense of place, an understanding to 'its character' which can only be constructed by linking that place to places beyond," as Doreen Massey notes (1993, 69). Massey's observation, which describes place as a node in a global network of relations, points toward a new "sense of place which is extroverted, which includes a consciousness of its links with the wider world, which integrates in a positive way the global and the local" (1994, 155). Asian diaspora poetry, in this sense, inscribes an interaction among different cultural passages, challenges the concept of homogeneous place, and suggests deterritorialized construction of new identity that is both local and translocal.

In the age of modern diaspora, place and memory are closely related together, since memory provides an important vehicle for Asian diasporas to link different places and to connect the past to the present. As discussed in the chapter on "Alter/native Stories of Memory and Amnesia," Asian diaspora poets express a kind of eagerness to get access to the deepest layers of their memories for stored cultural values and traditions. The yearning to remember their past has entailed an ongoing struggle against historical amnesia. What they regard as their Asian cultural heritages, in fact, is virtually absent from North American societies. As a result, they have to rely on memory as a means to re-store or re-story their fading past and to rebuild connections with their cultural traditions. Memory, in this sense, becomes an effective strategy for Asian diaspora communities to reinforce their original traditions and to strengthen their cultural cohesion. It is significant to note that Asian diaspora poetry gives voice to the unspoken, yet ever-present memory of cultural differences. As a counter-discourse to that of amnesia, Asian diaspora poetry sets in motion a mnemonic discourse that remembers and recollects the silent past from hegemonic oblivion. Memory, in other words, provides a wide, enriching landscape for the poets to relocate the deep dimensions of their identities, and to confirm their renewed attachments to their heritages which, in turn, give them the feeling of belonging, collective awareness and self-consciousness. These awareness and consciousness, moreover, do not merely yield an insight into the past, but more importantly, suggest a vision of the future.

In our examination of memory and cultural deterritorialization, we have noted that as a result of the global flows of diaspora, the location of "the exotic" is no longer confined to the remote areas far away from the metropolitan center in the West. But rather, the exotic has moved from the East into the neighborhoods of North American societies and become part of local operations. The chapter on "Writing against the Grain of Cultural Exoticism" examines the question of representing cultural otherness in relation to Asian diaspora poetry. Cultural exoticism, in a sense, is a "pre-condition" for Asian diaspora poetry, in that it had existed in the West before Asian diaspora poets ever started to write their own poems. Since Western cultural exoticism has developed a global epistemological frame in which Asian cultural identities are often the preconditioned versions that express Western perspectives, Asian diaspora poets have to rewrite and represent themselves in new ways; and their self-representations disrupt the existing paradigm of understanding and power relations. Asian diaspora poetry, therefore, characterizes an interrogative mode of writing in which various ideological appropriations and cross-cultural exoticizations are challenged and dislocated from their original meanings. Against the topos of various Western representations of the exotic, Asian diaspora poets have demonstrated their abilities to cope with the task of re-presenting the "other" dimension of their identities in a way that inscribes their own reflections on themselves.

Asian diaspora poetry has its unique features and characteristics which cannot fully be explained within the confines of Western poetics. In the chapter on "Styling Diasporic Carnival," we will address a few stylistic issues in relation to Mikhail Bakhtin's theory of literary carnival. In their writings, Asian diaspora poets often express a willful independence from and acute critique of the Western poetic conventions that fail to provide adequate forms for them to express their experiences and feelings. The search for appropriate styles to express diasporic experiences reflects a critical self-consciousness of cultural differences that may be directed to oppose the force of totalizing cultural hegemony. In order to express their cultural differences, Asian diaspora poets break away from the overdetermined discourse of canonical expectation through an act similar to the play of self-staging in a vernacular carnival. Parody, mockery, pidginization, slanguage and other formal experimentations frequently appear in their works, adding an extra dimension to Asian diaspora poetry that styles itself as multivalent and polyphonic. The idiosyncratic performances and experiments have special significance for Asian diaspora poets, since they provide a discursive space where their disembodied cultural inheritances are reconstructed into viable forms. The obsession with stylistic experimentation indicates a transgressive yearning for freedom of traversing various limiting borders. Artistic innovations and transgressions, however, are not purely formal, aesthetic concerns, but rather implicate Asian diaspora poets' self-conscious strife to articulate their cultural identities and values.

Asian diaspora poets are people with a double vision or a "second sight" which, in Robin Cohen's words, allows them to see "'how things are done' in other societies as well as in the one in which they find themselves." "Diasporas are thus both inside and outside a particular national society" (1977, 172). The double vision, which is reflected in their writing across cultural and national boundaries, challenges the totalizing national discourse by evoking extranational consciousnesses. It is impossible to obtain the double vision without detouring through other national domains or cultural worlds. "We cannot escape this situation," as Jullien notes: "there must be an elsewhere if we are to be able to step back. With it, our view of the question can be more global" (2000, 372). For Asian diaspora poets, the double vision has been incorporated into their dialogical strategies to deal with the relationship between the dominant national discourse and various counter-discourses that preserve rather than efface cultural differences. The search for appropriate voices to express diasporic experiences reflects a critical tension in Asian diaspora poetry, which signifies as well as problematizes the sociocultural conditions that facilitate an ongoing detour through different localities. Many issues discussed in this book have pointed to cultural productions and social structures that are larger than the political units of nation-states. Diaspora or "the movement of peoples," as Franklin Ng argues, "is one of the important themes in world history, but it is often neglected because of a tendency to focus on political units such as nations and states" (1992, 20).

The poetics of detour, in a sense, embraces turns and returns, ups and downs, paradoxes and contradictions in a process of circumnavigation. "The more we move forward, in fact, the more we are led to turn back," as Jullien explains (2000, 10). What we have noted in Asian diaspora poetry, however, is not the sense of an ending but the dynamics of constant departures. "We might conceive of the making and practice of Asian American culture," opines Lisa Lowe, "as nomadic, unsettled, taking place in the travel between cultural sites and in the multivocality of heterogeneous and conflicting positions" (1991, 39). The heterogeneous dimension of Asian diaspora poetry has broad implications, since the very term diaspora, as we use it today, indicates not only the "out-of-country" movement, but also the mishmash "out-of-culture," "out-of-language" and "out-of-oneself" experiences. As a manifold out-of-border journey over various discursive and nondiscursive domains, diaspora has found diverse expressions in poetry. Owing to its rapid proliferation, Asian diaspora poetry might be described, in Shirley Lim's words, as having "become a space for cultural contestation between forces for containment and enlargement" (1993, 149). What we need in the study of Asian diaspora poetry, therefore, is an "enlarged" or widened vision that recognizes and appreciates rather than reduces the variety of literary and cultural detours, deviations, diversions and digressions to a static position. The perspective of continuous detours will provide a new agent of perception or a "second sight," which can help us constantly reorient and readjust the angles of vision in our reading across cultures against an ever changing horizon.

Chapter Two

The Poetics of Cultural Transrelation

A Diversion of Identity

> A paradoxical community is emerging, made up of foreigners who are reconciled with themselves to the extent that they recognize themselves as foreigners.
>
> Julia Kristeva
>
> *Strangers to Ourselves* (1991, 195)

> Diaspora identities are those which are constantly producing and reproducing themselves anew, through transformation and difference.
>
> Stuart Hall
>
> "Cultural Identity and Diaspora" (1990, 235)

We
the migratory birds
are here this season
thinking
we'll fly back to our home
for sure

No one knows
which invisible cage imprisons us?
And the flight begins to die slowly
in our wings. (Kalsey 1990, 40)

Diasporas could be compared to stranded "migratory birds"—they are strangers from elsewhere who, without a sense of belonging, never feel at home in a new country yet unable to return to their homeland. "To come from elsewhere, from 'there' not 'here,' and hence to be simultaneously 'inside' and 'outside' the situation at hand," observes Iain Chambers, "is to live at the intersections of histories and memories, experiencing both their preliminary dispersal and their subsequent translation into new, more extensive arrangements along emerging routes"; for Chambers, diaspora is a "drama of the stranger": "Cut off from the homelands of tradition, experiencing a constantly challenged identity, the stranger is perpetually required to make herself at home in an interminable discussion between a scattered historical inheritance and a heterogeneous present" (1994, 6). In this drama, as we can see, the "historical inheritance" and the "heterogeneous present" are often transrelated and translocated into a diasporic discourse of global and local negotiation, which means both border-crossing and border-redefining in spatial and temporal domains, and which involves not only the crossing of geopolitical borders, but also the traversing of multiple boundaries and barriers in space, time, race, culture, language and history. Diaspora, which opens up new spaces for cross-cultural negotiation, creates radical effects of dislocation upon identity articulation. The complexities and ambivalence associated with diaspora have created a tension between two localities and a kind of spatiotemporal duality. It seems that diasporas have constantly to situate themselves in an awkward mediation between home-ness and homeless-ness; and they have to learn how to reposition themselves in a new relationship between their permanent residences and their "homes." This repositioning, as Julia Kristeva observes, serves as a necessary strategy for diasporas to "live with the others, to live as others," to be "reconciled with themselves to the extent that they recognize themselves as foreigners" within new social perimeters (1991, 195). Moreover, since diasporas develop multiple relationships that cross and span cultural and national borders, the trajectories of their identities, as a result, would occupy no singular cultural/national space but are situated in a web of social, economic and cultural links encompassing both global and local discourses.

After relocating themselves in a new society and culture, diasporas must face various political, economic and cultural forces that threaten their sense of identity as a fixed, pure and closed structure, which has been uprooted from its original territory by their border-crossing experience. Although diasporas may become "legal citizens" of their adopted country "through a prescribed, state-regulated path," as Katharyne Mitchell notes, they "become cultural citizens only through a reflexive set of formative and locally constructed processes"; in other words, "legal citizenship is not the end but the beginning of numerous, active local mediations over the 'terms of the local-global integration'" (1997,

229). The gaining of legal citizenship, in a sense, is one of the least important aspects of diasporic experience in view of the long process of adjusting to a new society, for diasporas often rely on their "cultural impulse" rather than citizenship for self-identity. Haruko Okano writes:

> In a house I do not own
> In a country of isolation
> In a land that belongs to others
> I sit on folded legs, bent by cultural impulse. (1992, 41)

Due to their new awareness of racial, ethnic, national and cultural differences intensified by their diasporic experience, a large number of Asian diasporas in Canada attempt to keep intact their original identities, languages and cultures. For example, one of the early Chinese diaspora writers, Charlie Jang, kept on writing in Chinese and expressed a deep loyalty to Chinese tradition. His works display an intense desire to keep distinct Chinese culture and values in Canada. Like Jang, many early diasporas, "bent by cultural impulse," attempted to set up an enclave culture in their adopted society and to build up cultural walls around their communities. As Garry Engkent shows in his story "Why My Mother Can't Speak English," the narrator's mother "feared that learning English would change her Chinese soul" (1991, 14). Although she has lived in Canada for many years, the narrator's mother refused to cross linguistic and cultural borders. The way of living as "foreigners" indicates a kind of seclusion that serves as strategy for self-protection. Under the pressure of being dislocated and treated as "foreigners," early Asian diasporas in Canada built cultural enclavism into a strategic shield to protect the autonomy of their self-identity.

In contrast to the early generations, the younger generations of diaspora communities are eager cultural border-crossers for they are concerned with articulating their identities over the borders of different cultures. In history, different nations and cultures often regarded one another as "savage" or "barbarian"; and this mutual demonization implicated an unconscious psychological projection of the self upon others. During the Enlightenment, as Kristeva illustrates, the "savage" or "stranger" was nothing but "the alter ego of the philosopher" or the figure onto which the thinker projected the inner self. "The *foreigner* then becomes the figure onto which the penetrating, ironical mind of the philosopher is delegated—his double, his mask" (1991, 133). Kristeva also argues that we are all foreigners once we are conscious of our differences. Thus, the recognition of our own differences transforms foreignness into commonality, "promoting the togetherness of those foreigners that we all recognize ourselves to be" (1991, 3). In this sense, the recognition of "togetherness" is based on the awareness of differences that paradoxically makes people come together with the realization that they are all different and foreign. This paradoxical transrelation between foreignness and togetherness has been represented by the younger generations in their search for new identity. As Joy Kogawa so well expresses it in a poem:

> once when we were rejected by each other
> (not fully rejected, not fully accepted)
> he said "We're totally different people
> what you need is a medieval knight"
> and he was a modern forward man
> scorning my reluctance to engage
> and called me untimely (1977, 56)

The poem, from which these lines are taken, describes the ambiguous feeling of a Japanese diaspora woman who tries to find love across cultural borders, cherishing a time "when the world was flat, truly flat/disappearance defined the edges of our circles." However, since the "edges" of both visible and invisible circles are something they must live with, they have to cross them constantly in their efforts to adjust to cultural, language, racial and national differences in their everyday life. As Robert Chang observes, "Although the border is everywhere, your perspective may render it invisible. It is through this invisibility that the border gains much of its power" (1997, 246). Because of the "invisible" operations of border at different levels, it is not a misnomer to call the native-born writers of Asian descent diasporas, since the very term diaspora, as we use it today, indicates not only the "out-of-country" movement, but also the invisible "out-of-culture," "out-of-language" and "out-of-oneself" experiences. The multifold out-of-border journeys over various discursive and nondiscursive domains—linguistic, cultural, national, political and economic—have transformed "a single time . . . into multiple spaces and tempos as the gap between words is negotiated, and histories are distilled into a specific sense of place and dwelling" (Chambers 1994, 12). Through negotiation with various differences, "a medieval knight" and "a modern forward man," as Kogawa's poem shows, may be translated, or rather transrelated, into an "untimely" formation of new identity.

Transrelation between multiple locations of cultures may suggest a cobelonging dialogue that situates diasporic subjects at the same time both inside and outside a culture. This decentralized sense of belonging, which develops on constantly changing configurations of diversity and unity, gives impetus to the production of hyphenated identities such as "Chinese-Canadian" and "Japanese-Canadian." The hyphen—sometimes invisible—seems to be so important for defining diasporic identities that numerous scholars have tried to clarify the myth that builds around this little symbol. For Lavie and Swedenburg, "the hyphen becomes the third time-space"; following Homi Bhabha's lead, they argue that this "space is charted in the interstices between the displacement of 'the histories that constitute it' and the rootedness of these histories in the politics of location" (1996, 16). To my mind, however, what this hyphen suggests is not a space but *spacing*—a back-and-forth movement that transrelates and works through different historical temporalities and cultural locations in the articulation of diasporic identity. In other words, the hyphen indicates neither a space of hybridity nor a split of schizophrenia, but rather suggests a path to untimely transrelation. The distinction between hybridization and transrelation lies in the fact that the notion of "hybridity" as a critical concept has obvious limitations, for it generates uniformitarian biases, obscures the boundaries of different cultures and temporalities, and blurs the dynamic internal politics in the articulation of identity. What I would like to emphasize is that the articulation of diasporic identity is a "mutual mirroring" process, to borrow a phrase from Wolfgang Iser, in which "different cultures are enacted under mutually alien conditions" (1996, 264). The articulation of diasporic identity is therefore situated in a process of transrelation between two or more cultural formations. What Iser has called the "mutually alien conditions," which challenges the model of hybridity, is essentially important for us to understand the politics/poetics of articulation of diasporic identity, for cultural transrelation is not a celebration of hybridity, but rather a quest for new articulations of identity that accommodate and transrelate cultural differences. As Stuart Hall argues, the "diaspora experience as I intended it here is defined not by essence or purity, but by the recognition of a necessary heterogeneity and diversity; by a conception of identity which lives with and through, not despite, difference" (1990b, 235). Transrelation, which is by no means a simple combination of different cultural and historical elements, does not mean to assert difference as an end in itself, but to form differences into a new discourse in opposition to totalizing politics. In other words, transrelation duly recognizes the complexity associated with the untranslatability of otherness or difference in articulations of diasporic identity, and includes otherness in the discourse of the self. The assertion of one's difference or strangeness does not only indicate the recognition of otherness in one's identity, but also presents a gesture to accept an extra dimension of one's identity. As Ramabai Espinet writes in a poem:

I am a stranger
Everywhere.
. . .
It is not for nothing
That we inherited a massive
Unknown and unknowable presence. (1990, 38)

Acknowledgments of otherness or strangeness in identification would lead to a better understanding of the self that can no longer be appropriated by means of autoreference. Cultural otherness requires us to recognize and appreciate the value of alterity—the "unknown and unknowable presence" in the articulation of identity. "The demand of identification," as Bhabha has pointed out, "entails the representation of the subject in the differentiating order of otherness," and "is always the return of an image of identity that bears the mark of splitting in the Other place from which it comes" (1994, 45). Bhabha's observation raises interesting questions about the issue of cultural signification outside its original territory. Since diasporic identity is defined across cultural and national differences, the noticeable otherness has become an inevitable "foreign" element of inheritance. However, the inherited otherness may give rise to a process of identity reformation in which the "foreign" is translated into measures capable of reinventing the self. Therefore, diaspora not only involves "mutual alien conditions" that challenge the traditional models of pure culturalism and nationalism, but also, as a result of the encounter of different systems of cultural signification, activates new forms of cultural transrelation that accommodate new strategies for identity formation by including otherness in self-recognition.

To a certain degree, cultural transrelation can be seen as a flexible strategy in identity politics for diasporas to deal with differences and otherness which can take on different configurations in identity formation and challenge them to face the complex interaction and interruption of various othering discourses beyond the essentialist, reductionist or poststructuralist conceptions of identity. "Let us not seek to solidify," as Kristeva argues, "to turn the otherness of the foreigner into a thing. Let us merely touch it, brush by it, without giving it a permanent structure" (1991, 3). In this sense, cultural transrelation is not to find equivalence in different cultures for substitution, but to expand the space of continuity in which various combinations and configurations of relations can be formed. In other words, transrelation accepts the increasing complexity in contemporary identity articulation without reducing it to rigid structures. In the case of diaspora, the experience of being the same and different simultaneously suggests a process of identity rearticulation in which people are transrelated into new systems of relationships. Moreover, cultural transrelation indicates an act of cultural defamiliarization whereby one may see one's own past and culture as foreign otherness. This paradoxical transposition between two cultural frames may cause people to re-view historical experience and cultural inheritance in a new context and to interpret them from a fresh perspective. Rienzi Crusz, for instance, describes his experience of re-viewing his cultural heritage in a perspective of changed and changing identity:

> The monsoon rain
> doesn't know me any more:
> I am snow-bank child, bundled,
> with snot under my nose,
> white fluff magic in both hands.
> Once, rice and curry, passiona juice,
> now, hot-dogs and fries,
> Black Forest Ham on Rye.
>
> So, what's the essential story?
> Nothing   but a journey done,
> a horizon that would never stand still. (1990, 24)

Cultural transrelation therefore seeks to compare and to connect different cultural elements in the articulation of new identities, which involves a dynamic process of self-revisioning. Identity articulation is not a simple combination of different cultural or historical elements, but rather a complex practice that otherizes and defamiliarizes cultures for multi-perspective examinations. Different from the traditional models in which identity is defined by exclusion or fixity, the model of transrelation calls for remapping new identitarian borderzones whose horizons "would never stand still."

Deployed as a description of cultural duality, the metaphors of borderzones, as Lavie and Swedenburg note, refer to the "sites of creative cultural creolization, places where criss-crossed identities are forged out of the debris of corroded, formerly (would-be) homogeneous identities, zones where the residents often refuse the geopolitical univocality of the lines" (1996, 15). Over the past few years, a wide range of strategies for mapping the configurations of diasporic identities has been established based upon the border theories developed by Gloria Anzaldúa, Stanley Aronowitz and Henry Giroux among others. "Living on borders and in margins, keeping intact one's shifting and multiple identity and integrity," as Anzaldúa maintains, "is like trying to swim in a new element, an 'alien' element" (1987, iii). If we want to trace the trajectories of diasporic identities into border politics, however, we have to follow Lawrence Grossberg's advice not to "view space as passive and determined" or "treat space too empirically"; instead, we should use "spatial vocabularies as figures"—"The figural language functions, often insightfully, to describe everyday life, social relations of power and intellectual work" (1996, 178). Although diasporic identity is often described in a "poetic language of travel—of homes, voyages and destinations," its articulation is not limited to geopolitical borders. The poetic language of travel, in Grossberg's opinion, only "reconfigures metonymical systems into synecdochal images of identity" (1996, 178). Indeed, beyond "metonymical systems" of territorial and temporal limitations, diaspora writers have found new poetic language to articulate their identities. In her poem "She is not a Fence Sitter," Joy Kogawa writes:

> She leaps over fences
> as if they've been built
> for no other purpose.
>
> She will not, she says
> stay stuck on a picket.
> It's the way of the scarecrow—
> it's for people who flap. (1985, 33)

Fence-crossing described in this poem suggests a transgressive journey that disrupts the constraints of borders. On the one hand, diasporas cross borders and fences to challenge outside limits in space and time and, on the other hand, to extend the inside zones of cultural transition and potentiality. Although diasporas may cross borders or fences in different ways for various purposes, they all have to renegotiate their identities in the interstitial cultural spaces. Moreover, as Abdul JanMohamed argues, diasporas are not "'sitting' on the border; rather, they are forced to *constitute themselves as the border*," since "the border only functions as a mirror, as a site of defining the 'identity' and 'homogeneity' of the group that has constructed it" (1992, 103). Articulations of diasporic identity, therefore, should be understood as "locales" of transrelation between and beyond borders. This understanding, different from the accounts of identity as unity or as hybridity, suggests that identity is seen to be itself divided and constantly in a dynamic process of transrelation whereby various cultural and national presences dislocated from their original places work into new articulations.

However, one obvious limitation of border theories is that the term "border" is mainly used in a geographic or quasi-geographic sense. Actually, in examining identity in diaspora, we should reconceptualize "border" as a temporal notion, for borders could be both horizontal between various locations and vertical betwixt different historical dwellings. By remapping diasporic identity in temporal terms, we can transcend the hereditary limitation of territory determined concepts of culture. Diasporas travel not only in space but also in time and, as a result, diasporic identity is not only multilocal but con-temporal as well. Con-temporality best describes a kind of untimely diasporic identity which, as Stuart Hall observes, is "formed at the unstable point where the 'unspeakable' stories of subjectivity meet the narratives of history, of a culture" (1987, 44). Hall's remark urges us to reimagine identity as a negotiated endurance among different time vectors and to reconsider diaspora outside its indicative mold as the antipode to a coherent cultural constitution. Central to this uneasy con-temporality is a paradox of being situated at an "unstable point" simultaneously within and without borders of time and history. Moreover, this "unstable point" suggests a loosened structure of temporalities that subverts the normative system of spatiotemporal imaginaries. For younger generation diasporas, cultural transrelation means to reconstruct cultural inheritances into an untimely presence of cultural con-temporality in the process of identity formation. The con-temporal dwellings of cultures are therefore shaped by a double desire to reinhabit the past and to reintegrate the flow of time and tradition. In their attempt to articulate their "untimely" identity, younger diaspora writers have to negotiate with different temporalities that criss-cross their ancestral "cultural gardens." Lucy Ng writes:

> In the summer there was the garden—rows
> and rows of vegetable greens, leafy clumps;
> long furred beans and tender-crisp snow
> peas, vines laced round the wood stakes you
> drove (the look of concentration) into
> the earth. Neat crisscrosses x x x x x.
> This is a Chinese garden x x x x x. This is
> a Chinese garden. . . . (1991, 164)

To cultivate an ancestral cultural garden within con-temporality of historical continuity embodies a wish to accomplish self-invention without losing cultural origin. By choosing to reposition herself at the con-temporal "crisscrosses" of different cultural traditions, Ng attempts to find new ways of transrelating the past with the present and to map the contours of self-identity in a translocal history of Chinese diaspora. As Yuan Yuan notes, "The self that emerges can be defensive," as we see in the early generation, "aiming to preserve the original cultural values and keeping its alienation and marginality. Or the self can be extensive," as shown in the younger generation, "losing marginality by mediating between two cultures" (1999, 300).

The idea of "extensive self" underscores a new consciousness of community that cannot be perceived only in geographic terms. As Bonnie TuSmith argues, extensive identity accommodates a sense of interconnection that may place "us in a different reality, a view of the world that is cosmic and holistic rather than compartmentalized" (1993, 122). The holistic view of con-temporality is crucial for overcoming the sense of unbelonging produced by the experience of diaspora and displacement. Communal dimension of diasporic identity, which suggests a transcending sense of belonging, cannot be confined to the boundaries of binarism such as *here* and *there* or *then* and *now*. In diasporic discourse, community is multi-local and con-temporal; so the term "belonging" means transrelation of cultures in time and space in search for a "collective"—a new and renewing recognition of togetherness and a kinship of re-belonging relations. As Jim Wong-Chu writes in one of his poems:

we met in victoria

we talked and discovered
our similar origins

you a village relative
while I a young boy
sitting quietly on the other side
of the coffee table
cups between us

we are together
for the moment
but I feel far from you (1990, 103)

In a diaspora community, people may feel at once "together" and "far from" one another, for the community itself is the product of a deterritorialized culture originated in yet differentiated from *fons et origo* of an ancestral moment. However, the "similar origins" suggest an immanent bond that determines and describes the sense of one's geospiritual (re)membership in relation to scattered cultural inheritances. The ideas of con-temporal and extensive identity find subtle exprcssions in Sky Lee's novel *Disappearing Moon Café,* which begins with the story of a young man of Chinese diaspora community who struggles through the interior of British Columbia, searching for the bones of the Chinese railway laborers. This literal search for the scattered pieces of bones reveals a desperate desire for a sense of "togetherness" of a dislocated and dismembered community. In their attempt to represent the richness and complexity of their identity, diaspora writers of younger generations often travel backward in time to their forefathers' diasporic experience in order to find a communal home at the unstable and untimely point where the past and the present meet. As Wong-Chu describes in another poem about his search for identity in an "old Chinese cemetery," the point of con-temporality determines the sense of cultural connection:

like a child lost
wandering about
touching   feeling
tattered grounds
touching   seeing
wooden boards
. . .

I walk
on earth,
above the bones
of a multitude
of golden mountain men
searching for scraps
of haunting memory

like a child unloved
pressing his face hard
against the wet window

peering in
straining with anguish
for a desperate moment
I touch my past. (1990, 105)

In this poem, the poet attempts to walk through temporal barriers to capture an untimely conjunction/disjunction between the "unspeakable stories" of his forefathers in the silent past and his own diasporic identity figured in the unsettled crevices of history. This poem indicates an awareness of cultural anteriority related to certain moments in the past and suggests the historical depths of identity in younger generation diasporas. The crossing of borders in time and history gives the speaker a new position from which to rearticulate his identity as part of the disarticulated history of Chinese railway laborers who have been buried in a dismembered past.

In Kristeva's terms, the unloved child's "searching for scraps of haunting memory" can be considered as a quest for a father(land): "No obstacle stops him, and suffering, all insults, all rejections are indifferent to him as he seeks that invisible and promised territory, that country that does not exist but that he bears in his dreams" (1991, 5). The search for a father(land) indicates a desire to go back where one belongs and to renew one's (re)membership of a communal home. In Edy Goto's story "The Dream," the protagonist, a Japanese diaspora woman in Canada, travels back in her dream to the world of her ancestry, the old Japan of several decades ago. Wandering through the streets of old Kyoto, she looks for her ancestors. This "traveling back" in time and space to a forefather-land signifies the ambivalence of diasporic nostalgia that is not merely a sentimental reminiscence, but a way of reinhabiting the past, a retrospective movement towards the past and back again. This two-way nostalgia often draws on the cultural myths, tales and symbols of an ancestral homeland, as Uma Parameswaran describes in a poem about her father(land) in India:

> In our ancestral home
> Every newmoon day
> Father, as his father before him,
>   in silk dhoti
>   vibhuti on forehead and chest
>   sacred thread dipped in turmeric
> sat on wooden plank
> facing the east
>   to repeat the purohit's chant
>   sprinkle holy water with darbha grass
>   and call upon our ancestors. (1990, 88)

To write nostalgically is to re-possess the past, to internalize a continual return to one's cultural root, and to rebuild it into a geospiritual dialogue between *here/now* and *there/then* in which new identities can be formed. The last stanza of Parameswaran's poem describes the poet's experience of returning to the present and characterizes a tension between identification with and separation from her ancestry. In a sense, nostalgia in Asian diaspora poetry is potentially here-and-now-oriented, and its effect is directed towards transrelation, not just recollection, of the past, for it suggests a journey to new identity, or rather to new questions of identity:

> But here the sun rises southeast
> And the planets are all a-kilter,
> And all my words questions. (1990, 88)

The location of diasporic identity, therefore, seems to be a traveling-back-and-forth that reveals itself as caught up in the space between home and habitat, between imagination and immanence, and between past and present. At the very moment of dislocation, the knowledge of an imagined and, at the same time, immanent community is essentially important for diasporas. Suffering the hardship of separation, dislocation and dismembering, diasporas strive to establish a new sense of belonging that is multilocal and con-temporal. It is with this mobile sense of belonging that Asian diaspora writers try to relocate and translocate their identities in a diasporic space beyond the spatiotemporal boundaries of national imaginaries.

The diasporic space evokes lateral cross-relations of transnationality and suggests a designation whereby the national belonging is resituated in a context of alienated extranational inheritance. Challenging the idea of univocal nationalism, diaspora asserts an extra dimension of cultural difference and a kind of "foreignness" in national discourse. Bhabha, in a discussion of cultural differences, writes that "the place of difference and otherness, or the space of the adversarial, within such a system of 'disposal' . . . is never entirely on the outside or implacably oppositional" (1994, 109). What Bhabha tries to question in his essay is the myth of homogeneity of a national culture. "Cultural differences," as Bhabha opines, "mark the establishment of new forms of meaning and strategies of identification through processes of regulation where no discursive authority can be established without revealing the difference of itself" (1990, 312). In this sense, what the performance of cultural transrelation reveals is something unhybridizable—an origin, a seed, a core, or simply a foreign element in the articulation of identity; and moreover, it is this "foreignness" that gives an extranational or global dimension to the trajectories of diasporic identity that figures in the unsettling liminality of national space and temporality. As Lakshmi Gill describes:

We carrry
our spices
each time
we enter
new spaces
the feel
of newness
is ginger
between teeth (1990, 33)

The "ginger between teeth" insinuates a kind of tension between the dominant national discourse and various cultural differences, which cannot be ignored in examining the articulation of identities in countries like Canada where diaspora has been a predominant characteristic of the formation of a nation. Canadian national culture, by defining multicultures in minority terms, reifies a relation of dominance and subordination; and for "visible minorities" such as Asian diasporas, mosaic multiculturalism means a center-periphery structure in which Asian cultural inheritances are treated as "foreign" festoons that would bedeck but never become a central part. In this sense, Gill's poem inscribes a meditation on the notion of "foreignness" that relates to the question of new national identity. The ever increasing heterogeneity within national discussion seeks the recognition of new identity that has been constructed outside the conventional national logic; and "by explicitly, obviously, ostensibly occupying the place of the difference," as Kristeva observes, "the foreigner challenges both the identity of the group and his own—a challenge that few among us are apt to take up" (1991, 42). The experience of diaspora as well as the increasing transnational communication in both political and economic terms has changed the configuration of identity articulations. Different nations have permeated into each other's spaces not only in terms of economy and politics, but also in terms of scattered cultural inheritances. However, mutual permeability does not always work out harmony. Caught between two different sociocultural systems that cannot be fully integrated into either one, Asian diasporas in Canada are subject to a process of constant transrelation which, in turn, produces identities that contain elements of foreignness, otherness, and something recognizably different.

Diasporic discourse has been a powerful force in uncovering the limitations and contradictions of national logic by evoking transnational articulations. It has developed a self-conscious awareness of its own splitedness and heterogeneity in its attempt to redefine the concepts of sameness and difference, and redraw the border of nation within a web of transnationality. As

Kristeva observes, "The more so as we are all in the process of becoming foreigners in a universe that is being widened more than ever, that is more than ever heterogeneous beneath its apparent scientific and media-inspired unity" (1991, 104). In this sense, Asian diaspora poetry can be considered as engaged in reexamination of the concept of nationality in relation to heterogeneity, for it has changed and reshaped our national consciousness. What diaspora literature shows clearly is that the "otherness" and "foreignness" traditionally excluded from national discourse have been essentialized as a productive part of new national identity. "Literally," as Gillian Bottomley observes, "identity means 'the quality of being the same'"; however, in the context of "the politics of culture within the negotiation of identities," national identity is "precisely defined across several imagined communities, i.e. defined in difference" (1992, 132). In one of her poems, Laiwan, a Chinese diaspora poet, tries to reimagine identity as a new land, a land "no one could have laid claim." By rejecting stereotypical images, the poet attempts to express anew diasporic experience in which con-temporal interactions among different historical, political and cultural discourses work into new forms of identity:

> Now you are here
> do you remember your syntax, your language
> that which would be the remembering of yourself?
>
> Here
> when you are told to go back to where you came from,
> tell it back to he who has said it/
>
> This land
> where no one could have laid claim
> no one could have possession
> still it happened (1991, 58)

To reclaim "this land" is to rearticulate identity in both transnational and transcultural senses. These two aspects produce negotiational strategies for diaspora writers to deal with the tension between the dominant national discourse that is based on a hegemonic culture and various counter-discourses that preserve rather than efface cultural differences. When reading diaspora literature, we can no longer continue to think of nation as a geographical or an ethnographic locality, and we must reimagine nation as a con-temporal body of interrelationships, where interactions among differential cultural inheritances transrelate various mythical, historical, political, and psychological discourses into an accumulative entity that contests singular cultural dominance by admitting foreignness of languages, alienated memories and marginal experiences. The transnational con-temporality established by cultural transrelation suggests a new, transcending national identity, whose configuration and liminality have to be reconsidered with reference to the manifold connections and interpenetrations between different nations that diasporas help create and stretch in cultural, social, economic and political domains. As David H. Kaplan has noted, "Diaspora communities give rise to spatial identities that are manifested at two geographical scales. They can be described as 'transnational' in that they are dispersed across several countries. At the same time, many diasporas are extremely national" (1999, 38). This paradox shows that the forces of different (trans)national elements may merge in a process of transrelation, which challenges the absolutism of a singular cultural dominance by relocating the site of nationhood in a diasporic space of global/local negotiation.

As Linda Basch et al. have pointed out, diasporas "simultaneously are affected by, incorporate, and participate in hegemonic contentions 'back home' as they learn new meanings and forms of representation in their new settings. They respond to and resist these constructions, and by so doing progressively transform them"; in this sense, diasporas can be seen as transnational agents who "have been influenced by local hegemonic contentions and global contexts, while at the same time influencing them" (1994, 16). This two-way process provides an extra or extranational dimension to the articulation of identity that requires us to redefine nation(hood). Owing to the simultaneous emergence of both globalism and localism, Kristeva opines, each diasporic subject "is fated to remain the same and the other—without forgetting his original culture but putting it in perspective to the extent of having it not only exist side by side but also alternate with others' culture" (1991, 194). By considering the production of Asian diaspora poetry as part of a larger transnational discourse—a discourse that has been contributing to the richness and complexity of the politics/poetics of modern identity formation, we may reach a new understanding of identity as the projection of our own foreignness. In Kristeva's words, "this means to imagine and make oneself other for oneself" (1991, 13). As nation is no longer the solid ground for identification, Kristeva argues that "the foreign" has become part of the self: "foreignness is within us: we are our own foreigners, we are divided" (1991, 181). To be "other for oneself" relates to a decentering sense of nationhood, since "foreignness," according to Kristeva, has expanded our personhood and nationhood that are no longer autoreferential or narcissistic. Diaspora, in this sense, has changed the very nature of nation and modified our sense of national identity, as Sean Gunn writes in his poem:

in the world today
Chinese
are people
who live in China

on the local scene
Chinese
are adjectives
that modify people (1979, 38)

Diaspora disrupts the apparent closure of nationality and invokes transnational interactions. Under such circumstances, the earlier conceptions of identity based on singular culture are no longer adequate to describe the transnational and con-temporal dimensions of national identity. What Gunn's poem suggests is the double writing of national identity across cultural and national boundaries, which challenges the totalizing discourse of a nationhood by evoking extranational consciousness.

It is interesting to note how diasporic discourse interacts with national discourse, and how the complex strategy of local identification is related to global, transnational consciousness. As a transgressive cultural practice that thrives on a process of constant resignification and recontextualization of established assumptions and meanings of conventional nationhood, diaspora has changed the context and concepts of national ideologies, national identities and national imaginings. In an age of increasing global interconnectedness and multifold diasporas, what was historically considered as national spheres has been diluted by transnational diasporic discourses. Nationality has been reconfigured in the process of diaspora and the reconstruction of identity of a nationhood often involves the mingling of multinational communities. In a book entitled *Post-National Arguments*, Frank Davey examines sixteen Canadian novels, and in the conclusion he writes, "One surprise in these sixteen novels is their lack of nationalist discourse and signs, unless ironically deployed. What they offer instead, repeatedly and paradoxically, are various discourses of intimacy, home, and neighborhood, together with others of global distance and multinational community" (1993, 259). This "multinational community," which calls for remapping the boundaries of a nation, can be interpreted in terms of continuities and discontinuities that mediate between the local and the global "where one might expect to find constructions of region, province, and nation, one finds instead voyages, air flights, and international hotels. Home and family reside not within a nation but as nodes of international" (1993, 259). What Davey tries to highlight is the international dimension of national discourse, as well as the transnational dimension of a nation. In Canada, diaspora evokes expanding interactions between global and local discourses, which transrelate various historical, political, and psychological presences into a new con-temporal construction of "post-nation" that demands and activates decentered transnational communications and communities where the local and the global encounter as contiguous neighbors. In Catherine Hall's words, "what might be described as a 'post-nation'" is "a society that has discarded the notion of a homogeneous nation state with singular forms of belonging" (1996, 67).

Asian diaspora poetry in Canada has represented an acute feeling of identity destabilization in this transnational world; and it is exactly this destabilization that rescinds any essentialist assertions for the patrimonial authenticity or purity of nation and culture. In this sense, Asian diaspora poetry suggests a loosened, decentered cultural order and national structure, and opens doorways to multiple configurations and diverse rearticulations of identity that challenge the overdetermined, canonized cultural and national discourses. In other words, cultural transrelation provides new sites for identity articulations that have to be redefined with reference to global and local interaction between different national discourses and cultural temporalities. Diasporas, in the process of crossing and recrossing borders of space, time, race, culture, language, history and politics, translate and transform a static historical nation into a dynamic multinational and transnational society. "The multinational society," Kristeva maintains, would be "conscious of its discontents and limits, knowing only indomitable people ready-to-help-themselves in their weakness, a weakness whose other name is our radical strangeness" (1991, 195). The formation of diasporic identity, therefore, is not a moment of transition, nor a time of combination, but a process of transrelation; however, transrelation is neither a carnivalistic celebration of cultural diversity nor a simple erasure of national distinction. Transrelation is an ambivalent process of splitting and overlapping that marks the diasporic identification with "radical strangeness" betwixt and between nations. Diasporic identity is not fixed or given, but has to be rearticulated in relation to each instance of cultural transrelation. Articulations of diasporic identity therefore depend on the transrelational linkages that are not built through the ready-made names, concepts, paradigms or theories, but through reimagining, redescribing, and redefining our national or rather post-national liminalities. What diasporic discourse suggests, according to Davey, "is the arrival of the post-national state—a state invisible to its own citizens, indistinguishable from its fellows, maintained by invisible political forces, and significant mainly through its position within the grid of world-class postcard cities" (1993, 110). This post-national "world-class postcard cities," as a metaphor, may suggest a new transcending identitarian nationhood, whose topography and membership have not yet been fully recognized or mapped in scholarly terms, but diaspora writers and poets have already dreamt it. It is in the poetic language of Asian diaspora literature in Canada that we find new articulations of diasporic identity that mediate between the global and the local, and move beyond territorial and temporal limitations. Let us conclude our discussion with a poem written by Roy Kiyooka—a poem seems to be written on a postcard from a post-nation:

Dear M.
let these postcards tell you where we are
let them fill in our silences. if
the rest of our trip has more of this in store
I'm looking forward to the Astonishments.
p.s. it almost feels like I've been here before . . .
but that's another story, another dream.
Hagi next. (1981, 18)

Chapter Three

The Politics of Re-homing

Negotiation of Cultural Dwellings

> A direct result of this race for speed that dominates life across the globe is the emergence of the migrant—the involuntary passenger-in-transit between cultures, for whom homelessness is the only home "state."
>
> Rey Chow
>
> *Writing Diaspora* (1993, 197)

When Rey Chow says that homelessness is coming to be "the only home 'state,'" she is probably thinking as much about the general condition of modern diaspora as she is about her own personal life (1993, 197). The poignant expression of worldly homelessness, however, is not a denial of the hope for home, but rather an assertion of re-homing desire in the age of global diaspora. Modern diaspora disrupts the apparent closure of home and generates transnational, translocal communications and communities. Under such circumstances, the earlier conceptualizations of home based on a singular location are no longer adequate to describe the new dimensions and transformations of home, which has been re-versed in diaspora not as a "felicitous space" of living, but rather as a process of becoming. In a sense, Asian diaspora poetry in Canada represents a paradoxical feeling of both homesickness and home-crisis, for the movement between multiple locations of cultures suggests a cobelonging dialogue which, by situating diasporas simultaneously inside and outside of a culture, intensifies both the desirability and the impossibility of a given home-place. As Iain Chambers points out, "wandering without a fixed home, dwelling at the crossroads of the world, bearing on a sense of being and difference, is no longer the expression of a unique tradition or history, even if it pretends to carry a single name" (1994, 4). In "a single name" yet a plural sense, home has developed on constantly changing configurations of diversity and unity and, henceforth, become increasingly contingent on the interaction of different cultural passages. Situated "at the crossroads of the world," Asian diaspora poetry problematizes the political nature and meanings of home, and suggests a dynamic, complicated process in which different cultures not only conflict one another but are also converged and convoluted together to produce new homes around "the simple axis of a mobility" (Kristeva 1991, 30).

The transfer of peoples and cultures from all over the world to Canada has generated an intricate transnationality and cultural globality, which are based upon the tension of interstices and overlaps of different cultures. The notion of home, as a result, has to be redefined in the liminal spaces between two or more cultural dwellings. The conventional association of home with a place of residence is no longer stable, since home, as Sara Ahmed observes, has "become separated from the particular worldly space of living"; and "the space which is most like home, which is most comfortable and familiar, is not the space of inhabitance—I am here—but the very space in which one finds the self as almost, but not quite, at home" (1999, 331). Our sense of dwellings, to a certain extent, has already been dehomed in response to the effects of global diaspora, and there seems to be no place like home any more—even home has become increasingly unhomely. As Lucy Ng, a Chinese diaspora poet, illustrates in a poem about her father's diasporic experience, home can no longer be ascribed to a pre-given site of location, since it has constantly been dislocated in the process of diaspora. As a result, the emotional, cultural and psychological identification is often related to the difference, distance and dislocation created by the substitution of "so-called home" for home:

> It must have been a relief after Hong Kong and
> Trinidad (mere islands) to find yourself in the
> wide expanse called Canada: British Columbia,
> thick fir trees, mountains solid as the back of
> your hand. You could buy a house, a piece of
> land, plant yourself firmly in the North American
> soil. Sometimes you even forgot this was the
> second mainland you called home. (Ng 1991, 161)

To identify a foreign land with "home" is to redefine one's identity against the grain of primordial limitations and to reconstitute home outside of the overdetermined discourse of native land that excludes displaced differences from the landscape of origin. Although Ng's poem makes explicit reference to Chinese identification of cultural ancestry with mainland China, there is an interesting and deliberate tension created here between the conventional metaphor of the Chinese "mainland" as cultural home, and the poet's invention of "the second mainland" as a concrete metaphor for Canada as the place of permanent residence. To make a substitute home in a foreign land, as Edward Said observes, points to an "unhealable rift forced between a human being and a native place, between the self and its true home" (1984a, 49).

After relocating themselves in a new society and culture, diasporas must face various political, economic and cultural forces that threaten their sense of home as a fixed and unchanging structure, which has been reworlded from its original territory by their border-crossing experience. The complexity and ambivalence associated with redefining and revising home in relation to diasporic discourse present a challenging topic for our discussion, since the very term "diaspora," as we use it today, indicates not only a condition of "out-of-country" displacement, but also the manifold out-of-border movement over various discursive and nondiscursive domains—linguistic, cultural, national, political, historical, has created a new homing sensibility—home has to be re-versed somewhere else, or in Nikos Papastergiadis's words, "Mapping elsewhere is also a homing device" (1998, 2). Diaspora hence refers not only to a movement from one place to another, but also to the transition that implicates a paradoxical, multilayered dehoming and rehoming process. Situated in an awkward transposition between "here" and "elsewhere," diasporas have to establish a new sense of home at the crossroads of diverse dwellings. As Joy Kogawa writes,

> For many years
> androgynous with truth
> I molded fact and fantasy
> and where they met
> made the crossroads home. (1985, 64)

Reconfigured between fact and fantasy, home is no longer a closed familiar place, but rather a dialectic sphere open to crossroads, or a shifting terrain related to far-away memories, or an ahistorical moment that has both passed and not yet arrived. The loosened structure of home involves two issues: One is the feeling of nonauthenticity of "home" and the other is the realization of the "home truth" about cultural imagination of "ghostly locations." As R. Radhakrishnan explains with reference to Maxine Hong Kingston's *The Woman Warrior*: "both the home country and the country of residence could become mere 'ghostly' locations," since "The home country is not 'real' in its own terms and yet it is real enough to impede Americanization, and the 'present home' is materially real and yet not real enough to feel authentic" (1996,

207). In this sense, diasporas have to re-verse home constantly in a "ghostly" negotiation between fact and fantasy. Since diaspora develops crossroads that connect and span cultural and national borders, home occupies no singular cultural/national space but is situated in a web of social, economic and cultural links encompassing both factual and fantastic conditions.

In literature as well as in popular media, diasporas are often presented as strangers from elsewhere who, without a sense of belonging, never feel at home in a new country yet unable to return to their homeland. Diaspora, which opens up new spaces for cross-cultural negotiation, creates a tension between two localities and a kind of spatiotemporal duality. While "most people are principally aware of one culture, one setting, one home," as Edward Said observes, diasporas and exiles "are aware of at least two, and the plurality of vision gives rise to an awareness of simultaneous dimensions" (1984b, 170–2). Constantly traveling along various routes, diasporas have to revise home as a journey through "simultaneous" mediations among different cultural dwellings. As Ben Soo describes,

> Prentiss be a traveller
> gathering the accruement of song
> and assorted parentage
>
> for an empire to be lovely
> you claim a thought
> to a sanguine family
> a coast of gold and one of ivory
> firmer transport takes you on. (1991, 95)

The "assorted parentage" implicates a decentralized sense of belonging and inscribes a tension of rehoming between two cultural shores—"a coast of gold and one of ivory." In her poetic collection entitled *Two Shores*, Thuong Vuong-Riddick, a Vietnamese diaspora poet, describes her own experience of traveling in a poem:

> Looking back over these years
> I see that we travelled
> from one continent to another.
> . . . .
>
> I went West, far, farther,
> looking straight ahead,

never looking back, until one day
I arrived at this ocean, the Pacific.

I stand on the beach
and the country I left behind is there
in front of me. (1995, 116)

When reading these poems, we probably should not view home as static. As Soo and Vuong-Riddick so well express it, traveling between two shores may suggest a paradoxical rehoming process between two cultural locations, where the home left behind can be found or founded again in front of us. Therefore, the process of traveling itself "involves a reliving of the home," as Ahmed notes, for movement is "the very way in which the migrant subject inhabits the space of home" (1999, 344).

Traveling from one sociocultural space to another, however, may give rise to a psychological process of foreignization, in which one becomes an unhomely "other"—a foreigner whose "appearance signals that he is 'in addition,'" notes Julia Kristeva (1991, 4). Diasporic subjects "with assorted parentage," in Kristeva's opinion, have to learn how to "live with the others, to live as others," and to be "reconciled with themselves to the extent that they recognize themselves as foreigners" (1991, 195). Designated as "visible minority" in Canada, Asian diasporas bear an unconcealable mark of foreignness:

My black hair is a dark beast's mane
framing a face etched in rain
(I defy your expectation
No, not pain)
yes, rain)
it washes away the expression:
Aha! She's Asian! (Gill 1990, 30)

Facing racial, national and cultural differences intensified by their border-crossing experience, a large number of Asian diasporas attempt to keep intact their original cultural identities, and they have come to terms with the roles of "foreigners." The determination "to live as others" reflects a kind of "aloofness" which, according to Kristeva, is "the foreigner's shield": "Insensitive, aloof, he seems, deep down, beyond the reach of attacks and rejections that he nevertheless experiences" (1991, 7). The cultural difference, in addition, suggests more than a "shield," for it reveals something "unhomeable," which is a foreign element in the articulation of identity. Actually it is this "unhomeableness" that gives an extra dimension to the trajectories of diasporic subject that figures in the unsettling negotiation between an old and a new home.

There are also groups of Asian diasporas who attempt to disaffiliate from their old home cultures; and their desire to "pass" in a white dominated society indicates the impact of acculturation upon diaspora communities. However, their disregard for cultural difference often makes them feel more intensely "not at home" with the personae they assume. As Vuong-Riddick describes in a poem entitled "Day and Night":

> During the day,
> I was
> the happiest girl.
> At night,
> I cried.
>
> My Asian soul:
> nostalgia,
> and sorrow unconsoled.
>
> You need to be a Westerner
> to believe in God's hand,
> the master of the Universe.
>
> Twenty years of Christianity
> have not changed me.
> An Asian,
> a straw
> at night,
> I am what I am not. (1995, 70)

The unhomeable foreignness—"I am what I am not"—suggests a kind of cultural duality and a tension between dwelling and indwelling, which calls for the recognition of new meanings of home outside of the conventional parameters of home identity. The experience of diaspora as well as the increasing transnational communication in many aspects of human activities has changed the configuration of home. Different nations have permeated into each other's home spaces not only in terms of economy and politics, but also in terms of scattered cultural inheritances. However, mutual permeability does not always work out harmony. Adrift between two or more different sociocultural systems that cannot be fully integrated,

Asian diasporas in Canada are subject to a constant rehoming process in which various elements of foreignness and otherness are reconfigured and repositioned in relation to new cultural dwellings and indwellings.

In Kristeva's opinion, the presence of "foreigners" as well as their visible cultural difference "awakens our most archaic senses through a burning sensation": "the foreigner's face forces us to display the secret manner in which we face the world" (1991, 3–4). In history, different nations and cultures often regarded one another as "savage" or "barbarian"; and this mutual demonization is based on the assumptions that home should be a familiar and unadulterated territory of belonging and that one would meet foreigners or barbarians only beyond the boundaries of one's home-range. In the age of modern diaspora, however, the situation has changed. "If we were to expand our definition of home to think of the nation as a home," as Ahmed observes, "then we could recognize that there are always encounters with others already recognized as strangers within, rather than just between, nation spaces" (1999, 340). To rehome, therefore, is to understand our differences and to accept new modalities of foreignness within home. The recognition of our own differences, in Kristeva's opinion, transforms foreignness into commonality, "promoting the togetherness of those foreigners that we all recognize ourselves to be" (1991, 3). In this sense, the recognition of "togetherness" is based on the awareness of "otherness" that paradoxically makes people come home together with the realization that they are all different and foreign. As Fred Wah describes in a poem:

> We are different
> from one another
> in the space between us
> a lot happens
> more than of only you or I
> . . .
> One by one one can
> become the other (1980, 96)

The paradoxical transformation from "one" into "the other" is characteristic of diasporic experience; and home coming in diaspora, in part, means the realization of the estrangement of home. Since diaspora involves a complex adjustment in which the mixture of various modes of cultural expressions has assumed an enhanced significance, the transformation from "one" to "the other" becomes inevitable. However, this does not mean a total loss of home, but simply indicates that an extra dimension of otherness or foreignness has been added to home identity; home, in "other" sense, is an interaction with a wide range of cultural passages. In addition, acknowledgments of otherness or estrangedness within home would lead to a better understanding of the self that can no longer be appropriated by means of autoreference. Cultural otherness requires us to recognize and appreciate the value of alterity in identifying home outside of its conventional mode. Since home today must be redefined across cultural and national differences, the unhomeable otherness is not only an inevitable element of inheritance, but also a notable mark of home as/in process. The inherited otherness may give rise to a process of rehoming in which the "foreign" is translated into measures capable of reinventing the self. Therefore, rehoming not only involves "the mark of splitting" that challenges the traditional models of pure culturalism and nationalism, but also, as a result of the encounter of different systems of cultural signification, activates new forms of cultural interaction that accommodate strategies for home revision by including otherness in self-recognition.

In the perspective of diaspora, home is not merely a place of origin but also a displacement of movement, for diasporas carry part of their home everywhere and translate it into various local discourses. The translation and transposition of home from "origin" to "elsewhere" present new expressions of home. In terms of diasporic subject, says Kristeva, "His origin certainly haunts him, for better or for worse, but it is indeed *elsewhere* that he has set his hopes, that his struggles take place, that his life holds together today" (1991, 29). The paradoxical relationship between home-haunting and home-hunting as expressed in the language of "origin" and "elsewhere" is connected to the politics of belonging that is negotiated in the liminal spaces of cultural passages. Different from the ethnocentric rootedness, cultural passages are deterritorialized and floating; and for that reason, the cultural code of rehoming, rather than that of home, becomes the primary signifier for the diasporic subject. In this regard, rehoming means to keep cultural continuity elsewhere and to engage in a continuous effort to write home out of the dislocation of life. What we witness is a mixture of contradictory trends: On the one hand, home has been diluted in the postmodern world; but on the other, the desire for home has been intensified ever more than before. Diasporic consciousness is hence predicated on a paradoxical process of home-haunting and home-hunting, in which diasporas may experience a radical discontinuity but, at the same time, they develop a desire for cultural reconnection—a kind of nostalgia for retrieving a home that has been lost in the past. Therefore, although absent from the cultural specificity of "this" moment, home is often retrieved or performed in the ambiguous mirror-space of recollection/reflection. As Cheng Sait Chia writes,

From the top of the hill
I see the city lights wane
in the glow of a chinook arch

My thoughts float to the East
where my village lies asleep
. . .

A note long forgot
calls my vagabond soul
out of the garish hall of this alien house
to the hearth of my father's home in the East (1981, 14, 26)

The village in the East serves as a mirror for the "vagabond soul," reflecting a longing, a yen, which gives shape and contour to a homeland that haunts the poet's heart. The paradoxical home-haunting and home-hunting seem to be a "mutual mirroring" process, to borrow a phrase from Wolfgang Iser, which "maintained the awareness of difference by simultaneously interrelating what was historically divided, be it the split between one's own cultural past and present, or between one's own culture and the alien ones to be encountered through a globally growing confrontation of cultures" (1996, 245). Mirroring "here and there," "past and present," "lost and found," home becomes a process of revisiting and remembering a plurality of experiences and connections that are reintegrated in the regions around the heart, as Evelyn Lau writes:

Once my father heard the monks sing
in a Buddhist temple. At home afterwards
he paced the living room up and down
singing their song
. . . . . .
I remember their song, he hummed it for days afterwards,
it was one of the last times
his eyes were shiny as bells, ringing
from some region around his heart. (1994, 44)

The "region around his heart" reveals geospiritual mediation related to the diasporic sense of home, which is engendered by and based on the changing mechanism of the international flows of various deterritorialized cultures. The "singing" here and the "ringing" there, at a subtle level, suggest a paradoxical interreference between two cultural dwellings that may cause people to review historical experience and cultural inheritance in a new perspective. The diasporic subject, according to Chambers, "is perpetually required to make herself at home in an interminable discussion between a scattered historical inheritance and a heterogeneous present" (1994, 6).

To make oneself "at home" in a postcolonial and postmodern world, however, one needs to exit into other dimensions of history, where the mediation between "scattered cultural inheritance" and "heterogeneous present" opens up new spaces for cultural rehoming and establishes new linkages between cultural temporality and diasporic subjectivity. For diasporas, home identification is always related to certain moments in history and traveling through the barriers of time would give them new positions from which to reconnect their scattered inheritance. As Lydia Kwa depicts in her poem, "time travel," in effect, takes on special significance and meaning in diasporic discourse, for it suggests a journey into "another's history" where "nothing will be the same":

> now the scientists are saying
> time travel doesn't have to be
> fiction anymore
>
> space
> like dough
> worked through by a woman's fingers
> ball stretched to a length, until the middle
> gapes with air:
>
> hole in time, through which we might
> enter another's history
> nothing will be the same again (1994, 26)

Traveling through different temporalities, as Kwa suggests, means to move beyond the conventional constraints of time and history. The experience of diaspora produces a shift in perspective or "a hole in time" through which different cultural temporalities are reconfigured against the spatial dislocation. Diaspora, therefore, should be understood not only in spatial but also in temporal terms, for it has, as Chambers notes, transformed "a single time . . . into multiple spaces and tempos as the gap between words is negotiated, and histories are distilled into a specific sense of place and dwelling" (1994, 12). In their attempt to represent the richness and complexity of (in)dwellings in diaspora, Asian diaspora poets often travel back and forth in time in order to reconfigure home at an unstable and untimely point where the past and the present meet. Relinking home with the diverse levels of scattered history hence becomes an obsessive feature of Asian diaspora poetry. Kogawa says,

> Forgive me.
> I am obsessed with history
> and always scratching for clues. (1985, 58)

Diaspora, which is usually associated with the notion of cross-cultural encounter, involves change, transformation and appropriation of cultural home in different historical temporalities. As Ahmed observes, we should "consider how migration involves not only a spatial dislocation, but also a temporal dislocation: 'the past' becomes associated with a home that it is impossible to inhabit, and be inhabited by, in the present" (1999, 343). Moving into different dimensions of history, diaspora has changed the existing paradigms of home; and as a result of the "temporal dislocation" of cultural passages, diaspora has disrupted old home structures and triggered them to take on new configurations.

The "obsession with history" embodies a longing for cultural reconnection that is embedded in the diasporic search for a home that assumes broad communal proportions in cultural memories. Communal home, as Bonnie TuSmith observes, accommodates a sense of interconnection that may place "us in a different reality, a view of the world that is cosmic and holistic rather than compartmentalized" (1993, 122). This view of home is crucial for overcoming the sense of unbelonging produced by the experience of diaspora and displacement. The communal dimension of home, which suggests a transcending sense of belonging, cannot be confined to the boundaries of binarism such as *here* and *there* or *then* and *now*. In diasporic discourse, community is multilocal, and the term "belonging" means cross-relation of cultures and border-crossing in time and space in search for a collective. Diasporas count on community memories as a source of rehoming that suggests a kinship of rebelonging relations. The search for cultural reconnection is related to an immanent bond that determines and describes one's sense of home. As Sally Ito writes,

> i am at my Teacher's house
> for my first calligraphy lesson.
> Grandmother has given me her old brush
>   and her old inkstone
>   and a blessing
> from her faraway Japan lips. (1996, 91)

Cultural reconnection, however, signifies the ambivalence of diasporic nostalgia that is not merely a sentimental reminiscence, but a way of reliving or performing home between the past and the present. Home, put in another way, is reproduced in diaspora and shaped by the desire for cultural reconnection, which often draws on the cultural myths, tales and symbols of ancestry and tradition. As Jim Wong-Chu tells us in a poem entitled "tradition":

> I grasp
> in my hand
> a bundle of rice
> wrapped in leaves
> forming triangles
>
> I pull the string
> unlocking the tiny knot
> releasing the long thin strand
> which binds
>
> I tug at the dry green leaves
> holding the sweet rice within
>
> peeling it back
> I begin to open (1986, 11)

Writing about ancestry and tradition, for Asian diasporas, is a strategy of rehoming that internalizes the continual return to one's cultural origin and rebuilds home into a dialogue between *here/now* and *there/then*. In this sense, home is a mode of traveling that reveals itself as caught up in the space between imagination and immanence. In response to the life of dislocation, diaspora poets attempt to bring home their own sense of belonging. In a symbolic poem, Kogawa writes:

> I stand on the edge
> If I enter the forest I am not
> If I enter the clearing I am still lost
> I move in a direction
> Chanting a creed, "We belong. We belong." (1974, 18)

In Asian diaspora poetry, the desire to belong and to re-member has been a central impulse to perform home that assumes not necessarily fixity but movement. The experience of taking home along in any "direction" the heart goes and of performing home on a move communicates a diasporic self-consciousness.

For Asian diaspora poets, home must be performed in a process of transrelation among fragmented memories, which feed them the sounds, colors and smell of a home that seems to be coeval with the totality of the experience lived and yet to be lived. In this sense, home is performable as a memory of a shared past that is already lost, but it also has the immediacy of the future characterized by the desires to have it, to embrace it and to live through it again. Put in another way, what home refers to is not a space of bygones but rather a mirror-space of memories that reflects the desire for belonging and for the destination of the diasporic subject. These memories might be fragmented and partial; however, in Salman Rushdie's opinion, "it was precisely the partial nature of these memories, their fragmentation, that made them so evocative for me. The shards of memory acquired greater status, greater resonance, because they were *remains*" (1991, 12). Through these "remains," home is relocated somewhere between memory and longing, a space betwixt absence and presence. Viewed in a broad context, diaspora is both an anti-home and pro-home discourse in that it affirms the desire for home but pluralizes home to the extent that home "disappears" in fragmentation. As Tilottama Rajan subtly expresses it in a poem,

> This fragmentation is
> The iconography
> Of a Time imposed
> On shifting focuses;
> A time moving
> In sections, sections
> Held in images. (1990, 86)

Home in fragmentation with its shifting localities implicates the passage of cultures that both legitimizes its production and undercuts its construction. Home, in diasporic discourse, can be considered as a proxy of both continuity and discontinuity where different cultures, languages and values converge, or as an unstable marriage of different traditions based on a paradox of constant separation and reunion. Owing to the transrelation of different systems of cultural passages, home may take on special significance in a fragmented space where different cultural and historical elements are performed into a new "iconography" of home not in opposition but in accordance to worldly dislocation. In other words, cultural rehoming duly recognizes the fragmentation associated with difference in the articulation of new sense of belonging. Home, therefore, should be inclusive rather than exclusive; it contains the elements of estrangedness, includes other locations, and embraces homelessness as its extension, for the value of home today lies in its power to function as a paradoxical image that, on the one hand, expresses process, becoming, plurality and, on the other, represents connection, relation and interaction. To rehome is to accept the many changes and transformations that have happened to what we remembered as "home."

Rehoming through cultural memories between and beyond the crevices of history acknowledges the dynamic politics of con-temporality that implicates both continuity and discontinuity between the past and the present. The ambiguous con-temporality inherent in diasporic discourse is often translated into expressions of the "untimely" connections that diasporas have to hold for a lifetime among different "place" and "noplace" of cultural existences. As Fred Wah writes,

> WHAT'S IT LIKE TO HOLD YOURSELF IN
> SETTLE FOR THAT
> A WHOLE LIFETIME
> NO TIME NO CONNECTIONS (CONNECTIONS)
> HOME UP THE HILL AFTER WORK LUNCHBUCKET
> EVERYDAY ANOTHER DAY
> EYES GLAZED UNDER THESE MOUNTAINS
> SKIN TIGHT
> NEVER WENT
> PLACE NOPLACE (1981, 39)

In Wah's poem, the experience of "no time no connections" indicates a kind of untimely and unstable home identity. His poem urges us to identify home with negotiable endurance among different time vectors and to reconsider home outside its indicative mold as a coherent construction. Central to the paradox of "place" and "noplace" is a desire to resituate home in relation to con-temporal cultural imaginations. In a self-reflexive poem, Jim Wong-Chu says,

> My father came
> from the rice fields
> to the city

and there he stayed

just yesterday
I sat and wondered
about all this

what does it mean

rice fields
a glittering city
I try to touch

both ends
are perhaps
a bridge
a causeway
linking rainbows (1996, 234)

To rehome is not simply to go home but to undergo a constructive homing process, to set up a causeway that can "touch both ends," and to reconstruct cultural inheritances into an untimely presence of cultural con-temporality with diaspora. The con-temporal dwellings and indwellings of cultures are shaped by a double desire to reinhabit the past and to reintegrate the flow of time and tradition. In his attempt to establish an untimely home, Wong-Chu has to negotiate with different temporalities that crisscross their ancestral "rice fields" and the modern "glittering city." To reclaim ancestral cultural fields within con-temporality of historical continuity embodies a yen to accomplish home reformation without losing cultural origin:

from green rice fields
to glittering city
the green and glitter merge

steadily quietly

outside my window
it is raining

today the rain

nourishes rice fields
nourish the city
nourish me (Wong-Chu 1996, 234)

By merging different cultural traditions, home in diaspora activates and nourishes new frames of cross-cultural interaction, which is not a simple combination of different cultural and historical elements, but rather a complex process that deterritorializes cultures for con-temporal rehoming.

Rehoming carries special meanings for women diaspora poets, whose works often present a strong voice in their strife to challenge the hegemonic, totalizing discourse of male-dominated ideology of home. Reversing home in their own ways, they develop a critical consciousness in diasporic discourse and adopt new approaches that embrace female-conscious counter-memories and counter-histories, questioning rather than celebrating the patriarchal values of traditional "home." As Surjeet Kalsey, a poet from Punjab, describes in a poem:

Sometimes
I feel like a female character
in an ancient forgotten Indian tale,
she used to talk a lot, all of a sudden with
some unknown curse she became dead quiet,
and her silence grew into a cancerous boil.
One dark night she went to a
deserted well among the ruins
and spoke into the well, whispered:
I've come to you as an ancient statue
forgotten, denied my stone body
I walked out of the ruins of relationships
and broke down the walls of tradition
I don't want to live death any more
There is life everywhere
        Nobody knows how to live it.
No pain, now nothing hurts more:
nothing can touch me.
        . . . and she left her words
hanging in the deserted well for ever. (1990, 46–47)

By examining the writings of women poets, we will gain a deep insight into the politics of home that has been complicated by the issues of gender, domesticity and sexuality. Diaspora across different political, economic and cultural systems, according to bell hooks, "requires the pushing against oppressive boundaries set by race, sex and class dominations" (1989, 15). In this sense, diaspora, as both dehoming and rehoming discourse, inscribes the changes and transformations of power relations, and unlocks new forms and expressions of home. For many women diasporas, home is a contested cultural process of being and becoming. Unlike their male counterparts, women diaspora poets normally experience twofold pressure caused not only by the experience of dislocation but also by the patriarchal values implicated in the ideology of home. As Himani Bannerji says in a poem entitled "To Sylvia Plath,"

> Sylvia,
> I was thinking about your death. It seems to me that
> you were done with fathers and sought a rest, returning
> to mother in that stove, that modern day hearth out of
> which life issues in the shape of food daily prepared, the
> brown warmth of the baked goods. The stove from its
> fixed centre draws the whole household. It is to this
> centre you returned, seeking to be lulled, to be
> regathered into that bellyshape. After all we cannot
> return anymore to the safe darkness of the mother body,
> to be rocked by the waves, barely hanging by a thin cord.
> When we emerge it is to the world of the fathers, strife
> gathers strength, we struggle and only in sleep return to
> that warm dark home. (1990, 12)

It is essentially important to understand that diaspora women poets confront double challenge in their struggle to subvert the patriarchal conventions and, at the same time, to re-verse home in relation to their diasporic experience. To rewrite home against "home" is a paradox that accurately expresses the challenging task faced by women poets. Many of their poems subtly describe women's difficult situation and articulate their frustrated feelings about sexuality and patriarchy. Moreover, some of them attempt to establish a counter-vision of home in their poetry, as they strive to incorporate awakened female consciousness into their efforts to rehome. Bannerji writes:

> I often think of her
> this thing called a wife

What is she?

I try to think of her
even as I am
a woman
a small limited form
marked by softness curves
hair teeth two giving hands
and a little resting place inside
which expands with need (1990, 3)

The study of diaspora women poetry will help us discern the deep connection between women's sense of home and their desire for freedom and independence. Careful reading of the poems written by female diaspora writers reveals that their works, on the one hand, represent their attempt to break the constraints inherent in their gender roles, and on the other, reflect their longing for self-fulfillment and freedom beyond the "oppressive boundaries" of home. Literary creation is one of women's self-empowering devices—that is, a rehoming practice that empowers women to assert positive identity, to gain a sense of satisfaction and achievement, and to have a feeling of "being at home" in their own voice.

The voice of women diaspora poets has become increasingly noteworthy in recent years, and their writing articulates strong negotiating power in the English language. Actually, for both female and male diaspora poets, writing in English implicates empowerment, since the command of English itself is associated with power and control; and one of the notable themes of Asian diaspora writing is about re-versing home in English which, in fact, must be remolded so as to express the specificity of their cultural experience. As Kevin Irie writes,

You've made the long
migration through words

to finally arrive, at home
with English,

a species of language
that flocks the world over,

a dominant breed. (1990, 47)

For Asian diasporas, to make English home is a complicated process where their "mother tongues" encoded with cultural memories have to be sur-rendered to new forms of expression:

> like you
> I too was mired in another language
> and I gladly surrendered it
> for english
>
> you too
> in time will lose your mother's tongue
>
> and speak
> at least as fluently
> as me (Wong-Chu 1991, 17)

Sur-rendering "mother's tongue" to English indicates an act of searching for appropriate discourse in a different language to express diasporic experience. According to the theorization of Abdul JanMohamed and David Lloyd, Asian diaspora poetry can be defined as "minority" or alien articulations within a major language (1990, 1–16). From their "minority" positions, nevertheless, Asian diaspora poets attempt to transcend the limitations of English by accentuating their own cultural sensibilities in writing, which signify as well as problematize the sociocultural condition of claiming home in English. As Rushdie says, "we can't simply use the language in the way the British did; that it needs remaking for our own purpose" (1991, 17). The use of English, according to Rushdie, indicates a critical consciousness, "because we can find in that linguistic struggle a reflection of other struggle taking place in the real world, struggles between the cultures within ourselves and the influences at work upon our societies. To conquer English may be to complete the process of making ourselves free" (1991, 17). Asian diaspora poets' effort, therefore, is not simply a matter of seeking to (sur-)render their stories into English, but rather to rehome and reclaim their cultural positions in a language that both denies and confirms their "arrival at home." Laiwan writes,

> The turmoil from war and opium and poverty
> made you leave your country.
> Exposed now to lands that will restrict your entry,
> you had travelled long and far to be subject to another's language,
> another's *syntax*. (1991, 58)

To be in diaspora means that one has to translate home from one language into another, from one culture into another. Home in translation, in other words, suggests a process in which home is re-versed in a new "syntax" of relationships that gives diasporas an alternative position from which to reformulate their (re-)visions of cultural indwelling.

The "examination of the concepts and structures we recognize as 'home' in the context of global English," as Rosemary George observes, "generates a reassessment of our understanding of belonging" (1996, 1). For Asian diasporas, cultural rehoming is more than an act of making a disappearing tradition survive within a mainstream culture. It seems to be a search for another kind of home and another mode of belonging beyond the boundaries of a singular language, nation and culture. Rienzi Crusz writes:

> Does it matter which way
> the road turns,
> there will always be another Grail,
> another son, another weeping.
> Wherever, the wind will never let go
>
> its secrets. Here on undivided ground,
> we'll fashion our own mythologies. (1990, 26)

Rendering home into different languages and cultures implicates a mixable and flexible rehoming strategy that includes various combinations and revisions of cultural passages, enabling us to "fashion our own mythologies" with othering discourses and to perform home "on undivided ground" between the local and the global. Today, as cultural interchange and exchange advance rapidly, the study of Asian diaspora poetry demands vigorous examination of the changing mechanism of the international flows of various deterritorialized cultures. In a sense, diaspora provides an opportunity to break spatiotemporal barriers and to open up new dimensions for transnational negotiation. Re-versing home in diaspora, therefore, requires us to redefine the division between sameness and difference, and to redraw the home-range of a nation within the web of transnationality.

Kristeva points out, "The more so as we are all in the process of becoming foreigners in a universe that is being widened more than ever, that is more than ever heterogeneous beneath its apparent scientific and media-inspired unity" (1991, 104). Asian diaspora poetry, in this sense, can be considered as engaged in the reexamination of the concept of nationality in relation to the "unhomely" heterogeneity, for it changes and reshapes our national consciousness. What Asian diaspora poetry shows clearly is that the "otherness" and "foreignness" traditionally excluded from the national homestead have been rehomed as a productive part of new national identity. In this respect, Asian diaspora poetry presents a kind of second sight that enables us to perceive some previously unnoticeable transformations of home within a "widened" universe, which has become accessible to the increasing complexity of cross-cultural interactions. In one of her poems, Laiwan tries to re-sight/re-site home as/in a new land across cultural differences, a land "no one could have laid claim":

> Here
> when you are told to go back to where you came from,
> tell it back to he who has said it/
>
> This land
> where no one could have laid claim
> no one could have possession
> still it happened (1991, 58)

To claim "this land" is to perform and to relive home in both transnational and transcultural senses. These two aspects produce negotiational strategies for diasporas to deal with the tension between the dominant national discourse and various counter-discourses, and to include the combinations and revisions of cultural passages without reducing them to rigid structures. To perform home in the age of modern diaspora, in other words, we need to break away from what Rushdie calls "a ghetto mentality" and to free ourselves from the "narrowly defined cultural frontiers" (1991, 19). When reading Asian diaspora poetry, we cannot continue to think of home as a geographical or ethnographic locality but, instead, we must reimagine and re-verse home as a con-temporal proxy of interrelationships, where interactions among different cultural inheritances transrelate various mythical, historical, political, and psychological discourses into an accumulative entity that contests singular cultural dominance by admitting foreignness, otherness, alienated memories and dislocational experiences.

Home, therefore, is not fixed or given, but has to be reconstructed and re-versed in relation to the increasing transnational interactions. Diaspora suggests a loosened, decentered home structure, and opens doorways to multiple configurations and diverse expressions of home. Through the study of Asian diaspora poetry, we will have a better understanding of the changing nature of home that is not only a place of living but also a cross-cultural process of transition and becoming. Diaspora across different political, economic and cultural systems challenges the overdetermined, canonized discourses on nation and home, and calls for the re-examination of how diasporic discourse interacts with national discourse, and how the complex strategy of local transformation is related to the global, transnational dimensions of home. Today, as Frank Davey notes, home has been relocated in the mediation between the local and the global "where one might expect to find constructions of region, province, and nation, one finds instead voyages, air flights, and international hotels. Home and family reside not within a nation but as nodes of international" (1993, 259). As a transnational practice that thrives on a process of constant resignification and recontextualization of established assumptions and meanings of home, diaspora has extended the range of home beyond national borders. Vuong-Riddick writes:

> I belong to a country
> you cannot look for
> on maps, in books, movies.
> . . . . . .
> I belong to a country of the mind
> with friends and relatives
> scattered in Canada, America, France, Australia,
> Vietnam. (1995, 1)

As the global interconnectedness grows rapidly, what was historically considered as national spheres has been diluted by transnational diaspora and what was remembered as "home" hence no longer exists "within a nation but as nodes of international." As a mode of transnational discourse, Asian diaspora poetry contributes to the richness and complexity of the politics/poetics of modern rehoming. Diaspora, so to speak, has expanded both our personhood and nationhood that are no longer autoreferential to a singular homeland. "The homeland is," as Papastergiadis aptly puts it, "for a diasporic sensibility, both absent and present" (1998, xi). Exactly in this paradoxical sense, the diaspora "is fated to remain the same and the other—without forgetting his original culture but putting it in perspective to the extent of having it not only exist side by side but also alternate with others' culture" (Kristeva 1991, 194). Side by side, differential global and local discourses translate various historical, political and psychological presences into a process that demands and activates decentered transnational home, where both the "original culture" and the "others' culture" become dynamic home-making forces. Under such circumstances, home can no longer be formed with the ready-made names, concepts, paradigms or theories; but instead, we have to perform home through reimagining, redescribing and redefining various splitting and overlapping cultural passages. In the figural language of Asian diaspora poetry, we have found new expressions and re-versions of home, which suggest not only a way of living but also a mode of thinking that transcends the discourse of nation, region and territory. Breaking away from the narrow "ghetto mentality," Asian diaspora poetry represents a reconceptualization of home as/in process that mediates between the global and the local and goes beyond territorial and temporal limitations:

> young ban yen had been thought
> italian in kathmandu, filipina in hong
> kong, eurasian in kyoto, japanese in anchorage, dismal in
> london england, hindu in edmonton, generic oriental in
> calgary, western canadian in ottawa, anglophone in
> montreal, metis in jasper, eskimo at hudson's bay
> department store, vietnamese in chinatown, tibetan in
> vancouver, commie at the u.s. border . . . (Ismail 1991, 128)

Chapter Four

The Problematics of Translocal Place

Cultural Passage beyond the Border Politics

> What we need, it seems to me, is a global sense of local, a global sense of place.
>
> Doreen Massey
>
> "Power-geometry and a Progressive Sense of Place" (1993, 69)

> The absolute is local, precisely because place is not delimited.
>
> Gilles Deleuze and Félix Guattari
>
> *A Thousand Plateaus* (1987, 494)

It eludes no scholar's observation that the increasing global flows of modern diaspora, which overcome distance/separation, have created the effects of spatial compression. In light of the shrinking of the globe, we need to reformulate the earlier concepts of "place" that are no longer adequate to describe the change of our sense of identity in relation to the expanding cross-border interactions. In this context, this chapter will make a few inquiries into Asian diaspora poetry in America, with emphasis on the relationship between the changing meaning of place and the articulation of diasporic identity. As mutual penetration among different cultural locations has dramatically increased, we need to explore the influence as well as the consequence of place-in-displacement on the formation of identity across cultural and national boundaries. With its ethnic vacillation and cultural ambivalence, Asian diaspora poetry demonstrates that the elements of different places may merge in a process of cultural spacing, which challenges the force of a singular cultural dominance by relocating the site of identity articulation in a domain of "nonlimited locality." As Edward Casey observes, "As deeply localized, nomad space always occurs *as a place—in this place*. But as undelimited, it is a special kind of place. It is a place that is not just *here*, in a pinpointed spot of space, but in a 'nonlimited locality'" (1997, 304). Diasporas, in the process of crossing and recrossing multiple borders of language, history, race, time and culture, must challenge the absolutism of singular place by relocating the trajectory of their identity in the multiplicity of plural interrelationships.

In the history of human diaspora, the question of identity is always tied to the politics of place. As Gaston Bachelard notes, the idea of self stands in close relation to the passion for place—"topophilia" (1969, 8), and the sense of place has essential significance in the understanding of human identity. Place, however, is not a stable concept, for the notion of place as a bordered realm or a narrowly defined point in space is obviously inadequate to describe modern diaspora in which place has been displaced and opened up to an undelimited system of spacing. Against Bachelard's topoanalysis, scholars in recent years start to reconsider the meaning of place in a new context. Place is no longer fixed or unchanging, but has to be redefined and renegotiated in relation to various modes of cross-cultural interaction. "The production of diasporic identity," as David Palumbo-Liu aptly points out, "takes place in a confrontation between two distinct time/place constructions, a chronotope characterized by atemporality and seclusion" (1999, 344). Under such circumstances, the configuration of diasporic identity, therefore, depends on the translocal linkages that are not built through the territory-determined concepts or theories, but through reimagining and redefining place in a new perspective.

Asian diaspora poets, who are concerned with articulating their identities over the borders of different cultures, do not treat any local place in singular terms, but rather translate it into a mixture of various cultural passages. In a poetic essay about the diasporic experience of his father, Fred Wah writes:

> I try to "place" you and the hand or head can't, try to get you into my mountains for example but your China youth and the images of place for you before you were twenty are imbued with the green around Canton rice fields, humid Hong Kong masses—I can't imagine what your image of the world was, where you were in it (where you always going home to Swift Current, were you ever at home, anywhere). How much did you share of how small or large the world was after we left the prairies? . . . Did any shape of such places ever displace the distancing in your eyes? You looked out at it all but you never really cared if you were there or elsewhere. I think you were prepared to be anywhere. (1991, 177)

"Place" in Wah's work suggests a paradoxical "anywhere" that challenges the myth of homogeneity of singular locality. Diaspora, in other words, establishes new meanings and forms of locality through relocating place in a process of deterritorialization in which "anywhere" cannot be identified without revealing its relation to "elsewhere." Wah's writing highlights two aspects of the articulation of identity against the changing image of place: the interrelation of different places and the elements of the extra-local that are paradoxically embedded in the artifacts of local operations. These two aspects are reflected in the formation of diasporic identity that both defines and transcends the local place. Diasporic identities, as Iain Chambers notes, "are articulated across the hyphen, the transition, the bridge or passage between, rather than firmly located in any one culture, place or position" (1996, 53). The process of deterritorialization does not mean the disappearance of borders, but rather it suggests the complexity and changing meanings of place between and beyond various outside and inside borders. Owing to their shared experience of mobility, Asian diaspora poets in America express a paradoxical attitude towards the question of borders which, for them, are at once barriers and bridges.

This paradox indicates a tension between different cultural localities—a kind of spatio-cultural multiplicity that both challenges and defines diasporas' self-conception. As Arthur Sze describes in "Every Where and Every When,"

> Is it true an anti-matter particle
> never travels as slow as the speed of light,
>
> and colliding with matter, explodes?
> The mind shifts as the world shifts.
>
> I look out the window, watch Antares glow.
> The world shifts as the mind shifts. (1998, 141)

The "shifts" described in Sze's poem disrupt the constraints of place; and they seem to suggest an excessive force of acceleration that transcends spatial limits. For the poet, the mirroring effects between the shifting world and the shifting mind implicate an emotional, cultural and psychological identification with difference, distance and dislocation. "We are condemned to wander—critically, emotionally, politically," as Iain Chambers describes, "in a world characterized by an excess of sense which while offering the chance of meaning continues to flee ahead of us" (1990, 12). Diasporic subjects, therefore, have to redefine their sense of place against the grain of primordial limitations and to reconstitute their "shifting" identities outside the overdetermined discourse of closure that excludes displaced differences from the landscape of locality.

Diaspora, however, does not merely refer to a wandering journey, since it enacts a process of mutual translation and interaction, in which place has been translated into plural interrelationships that bridge and abridge different cultures. The (a)bridging effects of diaspora require us to examine the spatiotemporal imaginaries of place within a new context, for diaspora informs of the multifaceted complexity of the dialectical negotiation between *here* and *there*—a tension that not only reflects the very nature of diasporic identity but also indicates a salient feature of nonlimited locality. In the age of modern diaspora, it is almost impossible to segregate any local place that does not involve non-local or extra-local linkages in a wide network. Moreover, what we find in diaspora is a dramatic change in the politics of place, which starts to redefine place beyond the historical opposition of *here* versus *there*, since to a certain extent, *there* has been both merged and emerged in the very characterization of *here*. "It is a sense of place, an understanding to 'its character' which can only be constructed by linking that place to places beyond," as Doreen Massey observes. "A progressive sense of place would recognize that, without being threatened by it. What we need, it seems to me, is a global sense of local, a global sense of place" (1993, 69). Massey's observation, which describes place as a node in a global network of relations, points toward a new "sense of place which is extroverted, which includes a consciousness of its links with the wider world, which integrates in a positive way the global and the local" (1994, 155). Asian diaspora poetry, with all its complexity and ambiguity associated with the experience of border-crossing mediation, suggests an act of constant repositioning in a nonlimited locality that bridges and abridges different cultures, accommodating to a trans-local mode of thinking and living. In one of his poems, Arthur Sze reimagines diaspora as creating a network—an undelimited "network of branching veins":

> In 1861, George Hew sailed in a rowboat
> from the Pearl river, China, across
> the Pacific ocean to San Francisco.
> He sailed alone. The photograph of him
> in a museum disappeared. But, in the mind,
> he is intense, vivid, alive. What is

> this fact but another fact in a world
> of fact, another truth in a vast network
> of truths? It is a red maple leaf
> flaming out at the end of its life,
> revealing an incredibly rich and complex
> network of branching veins. We live
> in such a network: the world is opaque,
> translucent, or, suddenly, lucid,
> vibrant. . . . (1998, 122)

To be in diaspora is not only to traverse various cultural and national spaces, but also to erect a bridge between *here* and *there*. In other words, the increasing global flows of diaspora that overcome distance and separation have produced the effects of spatial compression. As mutual penetration between the local and the extra-local has dramatically increased, we need to explore the influence as well as the consequence of place-in-displacement on identity formation across cultural and national boundaries. What Sze's poem shows is that the elements of different places may mingle in a network of cultural passages, which challenges the force of a singular cultural domination by situating the site of identity articulation at the intersections of various cultural crossings.

As a result of the encounter with different systems of social signification, diaspora activates the changes and transformations of previous cultural practices in the countries and societies involved. The transformations provide new sites for articulation that can be explained with reference to the notion of cultural overlay—a transliteration of different cultures. As Marilyn Chin describes in a poem:

> I am Marilyn Mei Ling Chin.
> Oh, how I love the resoluteness
> of that first person singular
> followed by that stalwart indicative
> of "be," without the uncertain i-n-g
> of "becoming." Of course,
> the name had been changed
> somewhere between Angel Island and the sea,
> when my father the person
> in the late 1950s
> obsessed with a bombshell blonde
> transliterated "Mei Ling" to "Marilyn." (1994, 16)

The notion of cultural transliteration may help us discern the overlay between different cultural spaces within locality and, more importantly, it highlights what might be called a realm of "deterritorialized culture" which, according to Mike Featherstone, includes "sets of practices, bodies of knowledge, conventions, and lifestyles which have developed in ways which have become increasingly independent of nation-states" (1996, 60). The notion of deterritorialized culture informs us that when reading diaspora poetry, we can no longer continue to think of a place as confined to geopolitical boundaries, and we must reimagine place as a site of cultural transliteration or a dynamic body of trans-local interrelationships, where the overlay of differential cultural passages contests singular teleology by admitting foreignness of languages, alienated memories and migrant experiences. Cultural overlay, therefore, suggests an (a)bridging practice which, as Lavie and Swedenburg opine, calls for remapping the "borderzone" that "goes beyond the old model of culture without establishing another fixity" (1996, 13). Identity and place, therefore, are translated in each other's terms, since "identity and place," after all, "perpetually create both new outer borders, where no imbrication has occurred, and inner borders, between the areas of overlay and the vestigial spaces of nonoverlay" (1996, 18).

When tracing the trajectories of diasporic identities into border politics, we should not view borders as predetermined in a geographic or quasi-geographic sense. Instead, borders should be reconceptualized as both spatial and temporal notions, for borders could be both horizontal between various locations and vertical betwixt different historical dwellings. By remapping diasporic identity in temporal terms, we can transcend the hereditary limitation of territory determined concepts of culture. Since diasporas travel not only in space but also in time and, diasporic identity is not only multilocal but con-temporal as well. As discussed earlier, con-temporality describes the "untimely" aspect of diasporic identity which, as Stuart Hall observes, is "formed at the unstable point where the 'unspeakable' stories of subjectivity meet the narratives of history, of a culture" (1987, 44). Hall's observation helps us understand diasporic identity as a negotiated endurance among different time vectors and to reconsider place outside its indicative mold as the antipode to a coherent cultural constitution. Central to this anachronic con-temporality is a paradox of being situated at an "unstable point" simultaneously within and without borders of time and history. As Lawrence Grossberg observes, "identity is ultimately returned to history, for one's spatial place is subsumed by a diasporic history and a colonial experience which privileges particular exemplars as the 'proper' figure for identity" (1996, 178). Traveling in history inscribes cultural memories that are crucial for overcoming the sense of unbelonging produced by the experience of displacement. However, the temporal and historical dimensions of place, which is closely related to one's sense of belonging, cannot be confined to the boundaries of binarism such as *now* and *then*. In diasporic discourse, the term "belonging" means cross-relation of cultures and border-crossing in time and space in search for a simultaneous collective—the continuity of a living memory across both spatial and temporal divides. In a poem about the early Chinese diaspora, Cathy Song writes:

> I have never seen it.
> It's as if I can't sing that far.
> But look—
> on the map, this black dot.
> Here is where we live,
> on the pancake plains
> just east of the Rockies,
> on the other side of the clouds.
> A mile above the sea,
> the air is so thin, you can starve on it,
> No bamboo trees
> but the alpine equivalent,
> ready aspen with light, fluttering leaves.
> Did a boy in Guangzhou dream of this
> as his last stop? (1989, 211)

The transposition of the Rockies and Guangzhou, however, does not indicate a geographical limitation of "the black dot" on a map, but rather it suggests "the other side" and "the other time" of this place. Viewed from the Rockies, Guangzhou is both so far and so near, and the multifaceted complexity of the cross-cultural community transcends the boundary of singular time and place. In James Clifford's words, "The empowering paradox of diaspora is that dwelling *here* assumes solidarity and connection *there*. But *there* is not necessarily a single place or an exclusivist nation" (1997, 269). Though he is dwelling on this side of the world, the speaker in Song's poem is nevertheless tied to his cultural ancestry on "the other side" of his life:

> He thinks when we die we'll go to China.
> Think of it—a Chinese heaven
> where, except for his blond hair,
> the part that belongs to his father,

everyone will look like him.
China, that blue flower on the map,
bluer than the sea
his hand must span like a bridge
to reach it. (1988, 77)

The "bridge" that diasporas wish to establish suggests a connection with extra-local elements beyond the immediate time and place. In Massey's words, "the identity place is in part constructed out of positive interrelations with elsewhere" (1994, 169). The location of diasporic identity, therefore, seems to be a traveling-back-and-forth that reveals itself as caught up in space between *here* and *there*, between *now* and *then*. At the very moment of dislocation, the (a)bridging knowledge of an imagined and, at the same time, immanent community is essential to their sense of belonging. To accede to "the other side," therefore, would be thus to enter into a paradox wherein we are always elsewhere from where we are. Locality, as a result, no longer merely means temporal or spatial limits, but rather it represents a regressive transposition—in order to grasp *here* and *now*, we must be *there* and *then*. Through access to "the other side," we are able to reconfront and redefine this side of our selves.

The simultaneity of multiple "sides" of cultural locality may produce a cobelonging dialogue that situates diasporas at the same time both inside and outside a particular place. This decentralized sense of belonging, which develops on constantly changing configurations of diversity and unity, implicates a deep dimension of diasporic identity. As Gilles Deleuze and Félix Guattari point out, "the coupling of the place and the absolute is achieved not in a centered, oriented globalization or universalization but in an infinite succession of local operations" (1987, 383). In diasporic discourse, the desire to belong and to re-member has been a main impetus in the structuring of a new sense of one's identity, which does not assume singular locality but rather plural juxtapositions. The experience of juxtaposing "local operations" with other cultural spaces is peculiar to diasporic self-consciousness. Li-Young Lee writes:

America, where in Chicago, Little Chinatown,
Who should I see
On the corner of Argyle and Broadway
But Li Po and Tu Fu, those two
Poets of the wanderer's heart. (1990, 23)

The juxtaposition of Chicago, Argyle and Broadway with Li Po and Tu Fu, in a sense, reflects multidimensional cultural passages between *here* and *there*, *now* and *then*. The articulation of diasporic identity, therefore, can be considered as a "mutual mirroring" process, to borrow a phrase from Wolfgang Iser, in which "different cultures are enacted under mutually alien conditions" (1996, 264). Multicultural passages, in Iser's opinion, "maintained the awareness of difference by simultaneously interrelating what was historically divided, be it the split between one's own cultural past and present, or between one's own culture and the alien ones to be encountered through a globally growing confrontation of cultures" (1996, 245).

The split within diasporic discourse requires us to reconsider the meaning of locality in a new perspective. "The concept of locality as a well-delineated and identifiable place," as Nadia Lovell points out, "is itself problematised in phenomenological, historical and political terms"; "Locality," she argues, "becomes multivocal, and belonging itself can be viewed as a multi-faceted, multilayered process which mobilises loyalty to different communities simultaneously" (1998, 4–5). In a sense, the multivocal and multifaceted discourse can be seen as a survival strategy for diasporas to deal with differences and otherness which take on diverse configurations in identity formation and challenge them to face the complex interaction and interruption of various othering discourses beyond the essentialist or reductionist conceptions of identity. The experience of being the same and different simultaneously suggests a process of reformation in which diasporic identity has been rendered into a new system of nonlimited locality. As Ben Soo writes,

> a broad deflection
> rough cottons washed to the grey of sand
> between meetings and dispersals
> of an excitement or ambition
> or the breaking of ties
> undertaking structures that respond
> in a different location (1991, 96)

The "broad deflection," to a certain extent, gives rise to a process of defamiliarization in which one's own past and culture have to be reconsidered as "foreign otherness," and historical experience and cultural inheritance reinterpreted in new contexts. For diasporas, locality is nonlimited, just because the "opening up" of place means to defamiliarize and to reacquaint different cultural elements in the articulation of new identity. Different from the traditional models in which local place is defined by exclusion, nonlimited locality links with "structures that respond in a different location" and implicates paradoxical overlay simultaneity.

Instead "of thinking of places as areas with boundaries around," as Doreen Massey notes, "they can be imagined as articulated moments in networks of social relations and understandings." Moreover, adds Massey, "a large proportion of those relations, experiences and understandings are constructed on a far larger scale than what we happen to define for that moment as the place itself" (1994, 154). In this sense, Asian diaspora poetry provides an appropriate case for our examination of "out of place" identity—part of America yet not American in an ambiguous zone of nonlimited locality, which calls for remapping the delimitations of place. Nonlimited locality, in other words, can be interpreted in terms of continuities and discontinuities that mediate between *here/now* and *there/then*, and it is indicative of the coming of an "epoch of simultaneity." As Michel Foucault points out, "we are in the epoch of juxtaposition, the epoch of the near and far, of the side-by-side, of the dispersed. We are at a moment, I believe, when our experience of the world is less that of a long life developing through time than of a network that connects points and intersects with its own skein" (1986, 22). Relative to the multilayered simultaneity, the conventional understanding of place as a consistent spatial construction is subject to renegotiation, since the concepts of border and locality as products of both ideological and geographic strategies of containment have been disrupted by the flows of diaspora, which offer new ways of fashioning identities between different cultural locations.

Traveling back and forth between different cultural locations implicates an unconscious psychological reflection of "the other side" of our selves—a "split vision" that makes diasporas aware of an extra dimension of their identities. As Russell Leong writes,

> I had split vision.
> In my left eye—
> a new village house
> yellow tiles, concrete block walls
> a slab floor without cracks.
> Running water, interior pipes
> and lightbulbs
> electrifying every room.
>
> In my right eye—
> a Los Angeles barrio
> red Spanish tiles aglow
> over a stucco bungalow

leaning from the last earthquake,
palm trees, taco trucks
smoggy orange sunsets—
At thirty times the price
of a condo in Canton. (1993, 11)

Traversing both worlds, the poet establishes a connection between Los Angeles and Canton. The "split vision," therefore, does not merely mean an awareness of another dimension of diasporic identity, but more importantly, it inscribes a paradoxical mutual translation between the two cultural worlds. Writing another world into *this* place is by no means a simple combination of different cultural and historical elements, since it does not mean to assert difference as an end in itself, but to translate differences into a new discourse of locality in opposition to the politics of homogeneity. In other words, the "split vision" enacts a kind of double-writing that duly recognizes the complexity associated with the displaced otherness and difference in the articulation of diasporic identity, and includes otherness in the representation of the self. The assertion of one's difference or strangeness not only recognizes otherness as localized within the self, but also underscores an extra-local dimension of one's deep identity.

Acknowledgments of otherness or strangeness in identification would lead to a better understanding of the self that can no longer be appropriated by means of autoreference. Cultural otherness requires us to recognize and appreciate the value of alterity within our locality. "The demand of identification," as Homi Bhabha has pointed out, "entails the representation of the subject in the differentiating order of otherness," and "is always the return of an image of identity that bears the mark of splitting in the Other place from which it comes" (1994, 45). Bhabha's observation raises interesting questions about the issue of cultural signification outside its original territory. Since diasporic identity is defined across cultural and national differences, the noticeable otherness has become an inevitable "foreign" element of inheritance. However, the inherited otherness may give rise to a process of identity reformation in which foreignness and strangeness are translated into measures capable of reinventing the self. As Diana Chang expresses it in her poem "Otherness":

"Are you Chinese?
"Are you American?"

I am fascinated

But other

Anywhere

So it follows
(laconically)

I
must
be
        Jewish

Leading to an eye-opener:
real Chinese in China,
not feeling other,
        not international
        not cosmopolitan

are gentiles, no less

no wonder
I felt the way I did
in the crowd

my Israel
not there

not here (1974, 135–136)

The complexity of "feeling other" and the placeless "Israel" that is "not there, not here" challenge the traditional models of pure culturalism and localism. Diaspora, as a result of the encounter of different systems of cultural signification, activates new forms of cultural interaction that accommodate new strategies for identity formation by including "otherness" in self-recognition. The experience of diaspora, in Chang's words, has created a "second nature," which entitles another poem of hers:

Sometimes I dream in Chinese.
I dream my father's dreams.

I wake, grown up

And someone else.

I am the thin edge I sit on.
I begin to gray—white and black and in between.
My hair is America.

New England moonlights in me.

I attend what is Chinese
In everyone.

We are in the air.

I shuttle passportless within myself,
My eyes slant around both hemispheres. (1983, 20)

The complexities and ambivalence of the two "hemispheres" are associated with defining diasporic identities among different cultural passages. Diasporic identity, to put it in another way, is not sedentary or fixed to a singular dwelling place. For diasporas, as Edward Casey observes, "dwelling is here accomplished in traveling. One does not move *to* a dwelling but *dwells by moving*." In other words, "it is a matter of a continual deterritorialization of the land, converting it into the absolute ground of an ongoing journey" (1997, 307). It is worth noting that the "continual deterritorialization" provides an extra inner space in which diasporas "shuttle passportless" across different cultural hemispheres, as the "thin edge" between dwelling and moving, and between self and other is blurred.

Without doubt, the experience of border-crossing can be viewed in positive light. As Edward Said notes, while "most people are principally aware of one culture, one setting, one home," diasporas and exiles "are aware of at least two, and the plurality of vision gives rise to an awareness of simultaneous dimensions, an awareness that—to borrow a phrase from music—is *contrapuntal*" (1984b, 170–2). Said's idea of "contrapuntal" expresses very well the simultaneous dimensions of diasporic identity and, at the same time, provides insight into the transformation of place from a static, singular entity into a shifting and multiple configuration mediated by both the inner and outer worlds. Asian diaspora poets, who attempt to articulate their identities contrapuntally, have to relocate their self-awareness at the conjunction of various cultural passages between interiority and exteriority. As Eleanor Yung writes:

Traveling through time and space,
whether in a car, on a plane,
sitting motionless,
I think I am still
while the world moves
quietly and
                                        tumultuously around me.
My stillness
It gives me tranquility, peace and grounding.
So I would like to believe.
But I know while sitting still,
the world inside of me moves quietly and
                                        equally tumultuously. (1999, 184)

Yung's poem points to an interesting aspect of the articulation of identity in diaspora: "traveling through time and space" in the world outside is related to the movement of "the world inside." The interrelation between the "worlds" shows that diasporic discourse challenges the totalizing teleology of singular place by evoking the inward dimensions of nonlimited locality. To a certain extent, nonlimited locality suggests a new way to explore deeply how diasporas cope with the inside tumultuous tension between a dominant teleology that is based on a hegemonic culture and the various counter-discourses that preserve rather than efface cultural differences within locality.

To a certain degree, inward traveling can be seen as a flexible strategy in identity politics for diasporas to deal with differences and otherness, which may take on different configurations in identity formation and challenge them to face the complex interaction and interruption of various othering discourses beyond the external limitations of identity. As Eleanor Yung says,

You have all the time in the world.
There is no limit, no end, no hurry.
Simply be here, be your essential you.
I am going to be quiet for a while.
There will be silence.
Listen to the silence inside yourself. (1999, 186)

Diasporic identity, so to speak, is a process of inward traveling, since diasporas have other places within them that transcend the outside place. Through inward traveling, diasporas are detached from what is present, yet at the same time, they are constantly delivered back to the present. Inward traveling, to be exact, is not to find another place in different cultures for substitution, but to expand the copresence of inner and outer worlds in which various combinations and configurations of cross-cultural relations can be formed. In other words, to describe locality as nonlimited means to accept the copresence of different worlds that accommodates to the increasing complexity in con-temporal identity articulation without reducing it to rigid structures.

In the case of diaspora, the experience of being the same and different simultaneously suggests a process of identity (re)formation in which both the inner and outer worlds are translated into new systems of relationships. Moreover, the inward-looking perspective implicates an act of cultural defamiliarization whereby one may see one's own past and culture as foreign otherness. To "shuttle passportless" between different cultural spheres may cause people to re-view historical experience and cultural inheritance in a new context and to understand the extra dimensions of diasporic identity. The outer border-crossing movements and the inner expression of cultural differences are actually related together in the process of diaspora. As Jacques Derrida says, "outer edge or border can also be considered an inner fold" (1979, 76). The "inner fold" suggests an ambiguous feeling of diasporas who try to find some "seed element" in their identities. Mei-Mei Berssenbrugge writes,

> Use crystals to identify this seed element introduced into my body, as if by genetic index.
>
> Matter becomes a matter of my expression.
>
> A fold in matter relates to the light of memory, the way the fold catches illumination and varies, according to the light of day.
>
> How does a fold itself determine "thin" and superimposable depth, the paper fold defining a "minimum" of depth on our scale, as the image of a pleated fan casts a sense of depth in front of the image of a wall? (1998, 74)

In a symbolic sense, the "fold catches illumination," because diaspora is a process in which both visible and invisible edges are folded like "a pleated fan" that "casts a sense of depth" across different worlds. Diasporic subjects, so to say, have to traverse various "walls," thin or thick, in their efforts to adjust cultural, language, racial and national differences. In the process of crossing borders or walls into a new world, the "inner fold" may indicate a new sense of place that is both "separating" and "connecting" us. As Sharon Hom describes:

I am moving towards you, away from you.
Simultaneously. We are breathing
Inhaling and exhaling long even breaths
ten thousand miles of dreamtime
separating us, connecting us
The sudden sharp daylight
through the closed shades
Exposing Time's contingency. Again and again.
I am back. I am gone. At the Horizon's shifting edges. (1999, 144)

Central to the inner fold of borders is a desire to situate oneself beyond the "closed shades" of "time's contingency," and to redefine place outside its conventional indicative mold. Across the "shifting edges" of the world, diaspora suggests a special sense of place in relation to the loosened structure of nonlimited locality that subverts the normative system of spatiotemporal restrictions.

After relocating themselves in a new society and culture, diasporas must experience deterritorializations of many kinds, ranging from political to cultural displacement, which threaten their sense of identity as a fixed, pure and closed structure. Due to their new awareness of racial, ethnic, national and cultural differences intensified by their diasporic experience, a large number of Asian diasporas may feel they have become more "Asian" than they were in their original countries, since cultural characteristics may become more conspicuous across borders than within their own territories. As Zhang Zhen writes,

The nature of this place
is a bad fit with my past,
yet sometimes I glimpse
my life's other half.

Sometimes I can think back far:
the aged thorn trees and stone steps
force me to consider:
should I be buried in this foreign land

or drift back like white rain
and drop into the lake of my hometown? (1999, 102)

This poem suggests an "inner folding" of border effects between "this place" and that "hometown," which accompanies the experience of identity disorientation in diaspora. In a recent study, David Johnson and Scott Michaelsen have discussed the "the complex of border effects." In response to the question of the "inner folding" of borders, they point out that border effects "involve the sensing of relationality *interpreted* as an exterior completeness and totality that, at one and the same time, *feels* interiorized—and this can be understood as the largest possible but still phantom effect of the project of bordering" (1997, 15). In this sense, diaspora facilitates the production of new identity expressions, highlighting "life's other half" by establishing trans-local positionalities. Johnsen and Michaelsen argue that "It is a version of the 'border effect' that produces a sense of individual cultural completeness, logically extended to its maximum—to the culture that is the combination of all independent cultures" (1997, 15). Since diaspora gives rise to the production of multifaceted forms, the cultural conflicts and ambiguities inherent in diasporic experience are inevitable expressions of new identities over differences. The overwhelming experiences of disorientation and displacement, to a certain extent, provide new sites for diasporas to rearticulate their complete identities across the borders of various "independent cultures."

As diasporic subjects come into different sociopolitical systems, they bring with them their traditional values and beliefs that may not be compatible with existing schemes of knowledge and power relations. As a result, diaspora becomes a transformative process in which old power relations must be readjusted and various cultural and national elements displaced from their original positions are formed into new articulations, which do not necessarily produce harmonious hybridity. Actually, the tension between various cultural differences often lies at the very heart of Asian diaspora poetry. As Li-Young Lee writes:

> I can hear in your voice
> you were born in one country
> and will die in another,
>
> and where you live is where you'll be buried,
> and when you dream it's where you were born,
>
> and the moon never hangs in both skies
> on the same night,
>
> and that's why you think the moon has a sister,
> that's why your day is hostage to your nights. (2001, 58)

Diasporic discourse, as Lee so well expresses it, implicates a longing for trans-local connections with another cultural dwelling:

> And when you close your eyes
> you can hear the ancient fountains
> from which they derive. (2001, 60)

Reading Lee's poem, we may note a tension as well as a linkage between different cultural spaces. The tension is created through the linkage that redefines place beyond borders and translates it into a new strategy for cross-cultural negotiation. It indicates a two-way process which, as Mary Louise Pratt has imagined, is "transforming the way literature and culture are conceived." It is both the process and product of globalization: "The increased integration of the planet, the increasingly rapid flows of people, information, money, commodities, and cultural production, and the changes of consciousness which result" (1995, 59). In this sense, diasporas can be seen as trans-local agents who have been influenced by and influencing global/local integration at the same time.

For diasporas, the articulation of identity means a constant trans-local negotiation between cultures. According to Hamid Naficy, diasporas can be described as "interstitial creatures, liminars suffused with hybrid excess"; therefore, their identities accommodate a paradox: "On the one hand, like Derrida's 'undecidables' they can be 'both and neither'"; "On the other hand, they could aptly be called, in Rushdie's words, 'at once plural and partial'" (1996, 125). This paradox has been illustrated in Asian diaspora poetry; and it shows that the forces of different trans-local elements may merge with local discourse to challenge the absolutism of a singular cultural dominance by relocating the site of identity at the intersection of plural interrelationships. The complexities and ambivalence associated with diaspora have created a fold of multiple localities and a kind of spatiotemporal simultaneity. It seems that diasporas have constantly to situate themselves in a paradoxical discourse of "discrepancies," as Li-Young Lee writes:

> We've moved into a bigger house.
> Now our voices wander among the rooms
> calling, *Where are you?*
>
> And what we can't forget
> of other houses confuses us
> as we answer back and forth, *Over here*!

> It's a little like returning to the village
> where you were born, the sad bewilderment
> of discrepancies between
> what you remember and what's there. (2001, 22)

This symbolic poem highlights the "bewilderment of discrepancies," as diaspora opens up new spaces for cross-cultural negotiation, in which place has radically been transformed and translated into a new house/system of relations. "To come from elsewhere, from 'there' not 'here,' and hence to be simultaneously 'inside' and 'outside' the situation at hand," observes Iain Chambers, "is to live at the intersections of histories and memories" (1994, 6). These intersections, moreover, are often enacted in a discourse of cross-cultural negotiation that gives an extra dimension to the trajectory of diasporic identity that figures over unsettling borders.

Chambers's observation highlights the complexity and multiplicity of border-crossing experiences. On the one hand, diasporas cross borders to challenge outside limits in space and, on the other hand, to extend the inside zones of cultural transition and potentiality. Although diasporas may cross borders in different ways for various purposes, they all have to renegotiate their identities in the interstitial cultural spaces. Articulations of diasporic identity, therefore, can be understood as locales of different cultural passages between and beyond borders. This understanding, different from the accounts of identity as unity or as hybridity, suggests that diasporic identity should be examined in a process of dynamic regression in which various cultural and national presences dislocated from their original sites work into new expressions. In this sense, Asian diaspora poets can be described as "border intellectuals" who, as Abdul JanMohamed notes, are "able to combine elements of the two cultures in order to articulate new syncretic forms and experiences" (1992, 97).

Diaspora, therefore, means both border-crossing and border-redefining in spatial and temporal domains, and it involves not only the crossing of geopolitical borders, but also the traversing of multiple boundaries and barriers in space, time, race, culture, language, history, and politics. Diaspora, which opens up new spaces for cross-cultural negotiation, creates radical effects of dislocation upon identity articulation. Since diaspora develops multiple relationships that cross and span various borders, the trajectories of diasporic identity, as a result, occupy no singular place but are situated in a complex network of social, cultural and psychological links encompassing both local and extra-local discourses. According to Massey, place and identity are no longer determined only by some locally originated, singular force, but also by the multiplicity of criss-crossing linkages to the "outside." "Definition," Massey opines, "does not have to be through simple counterposition to the outside; it can come, in part, precisely through the particularity of linkage to that 'outside' which is therefore itself part of what constitutes the place" (1994, 155). To a certain extent, place and identity are in the process of "opening up," as extra-local and trans-local elements have been both merged and emerged in the very characterization of locality. In the age of modern diaspora, interconnectivity seems to become part of our every day life and the common practice of identity articulation. As cultural mutual penetration becomes an important characteristic of our epoch, it is increasingly difficult to draw the division between *here* and *there*, between inside and outside, and between the local and the extra-local. For diasporas, "there is no intermediary distance, or all distance is intermediary," as Deleuze and Guattari point out; "the absolute is local, precisely because place is not delimited" (1987, 494). Modern diaspora, in this sense, evokes an interaction among different cultural passages, challenges homogeneous mode of belonging, and suggests deterritorialized construction of new identity that is both immediately local and yet mediated by the wide world. Diasporic identity, therefore, can be considered as a movement that is not circumscribed by any singular place, as it is inscribed in a never-finished process of traveling:

> Did Columbus know there'd be an end to all
> his travels—did he expect to find
> a new world? Picture him washed up on a shelf
> of sand, blazing forth again! I wish
> I could be like him and somehow keep myself
> alive, leave the last word unfinished. (Liu 1992, 12)

Chapter Five

Alter/native Stories of Memory and Amnesia

A Mnemonic Inquiry

Remembering goes on and we go on with it; we could not go on without it even if we do not make it or control it.

Edward S. Casey

Remembering (1987, 311)

More than blood, it is memory that confers identity on an ethnic group and sustains life.

Stephen Bertman

Cultural Amnesia (2000, 52)

That half is almost gone,
the Chinese half,
the fair side of a peach,
darkened by the knife of time,
fades like a cruel sun.

In my thirtieth year
I wrote a letter to my mother.

I had forgotten the character
for "love." I remember vaguely
the radical "heart."

The ancestors won't fail to remind you
the vital and vestigial organs
where the emotions come from. (Chin 2002, 17)

Related to Marilyn Chin's anguish over the "half" of her self that "is almost gone" are the entangled issues of memory and identity. "We are made of our memories" (1987, 290), as Edward Casey points out. In this sense, the study of identity must involve the examination of what we have remembered as well as what we have forgotten. In the process of diaspora, owing to temporal, geographical and cultural dislocation, some "fair sides" of Asian diasporas' original languages, traditions and customs might have faded and become increasingly intangible. But paradoxically, cultural memory, however vague, is essentially significant for Asian diasporas' efforts to understand themselves and to articulate their identities. It is like a whisper from the subliminal depths that has survived the effects of historical amnesia to remind them of who they are, and it involves conscious and unconscious assumptions about certain dimensions of their cultural knowledge and emotional experiences.

Memories of the past are associated with a deeply-rooted consciousness that may have been obscured by layers upon layers of ideological beliefs and practices in contemporary societies. Our attitudes towards memory reflect not only our understandings of the past but also our ideas about ourselves today. As James Fentress and Chris Wickham contend, "a study of the way we remember is a study of the way we are" (1992, 7). Memory, so to speak, provides an apposite position for us to articulate identity in relation to our past. In his poem "The Past," Ha Jin tells us:

> I have supposed my past is a part of myself.
> As my shadow appears whenever I'm in the sun
> the past cannot be thrown off and its weight
> must be borne, or I will become another man. (1996, 63)

The past is described as "part" of the speaker's self, which is kept alive by memories—as Michael Lambek observes, "alive in the sense that it continues to provoke a series of positions from which to interpret the present; and alive in the sense that it is not fixed or stagnant but can acquiesce to change" (2003, 206). The past, nevertheless, can be relived and reconnected to the present in different ways:

> But I saw someone wall his past into a garden
> whose produce is always in fashion
> If you enter his property without permission
> He will welcome you with a watchdog or a gun.
>
> I saw someone set up his past as a harbor.

Wherever it sails, his boat is safe—
if a storm comes, he can always head for home.
His voyage is the adventure of a kite.

I saw someone drop his past like trash.
He buried it and shed it altogether.
He has shown me that without the past
one can also move ahead and get somewhere.

Like a shroud my past surrounds me,
but I will cut it and stitch it,
to make good shoes with it,
shoes that fit my feet. (1996, 63)

For Asian diasporas, memory appears to be particularly important, because they rely on it for the development of self-realization and community solidarity. As the last stanza of Ha Jin's poem indicates, memory of the past suggests a process of self-making, in which the speaker would follow his own ways to "cut" and "stitch" the past, shaping it into new self-representations.

What Ha Jin's poem shows is a figuration of the self as a carrier of cultural memory, whose identity is defined by these memory resources. From this perspective, we can understand that memory functions to provide a workable position for the creation of a coherent identity. Since the Renaissance times, memory has been considered as "the seat of identity." As William West asserts, "while reason made one human, it was memory that made one a particular individual" (2003, 62). Today, however, the situation has become much more complicated for Asian diasporas in North America, since memory implicates not only a "seat" of their self-consciousnesses, but also a collective realm for cultural preservation in a society where the social system of beliefs and practices constantly efface and erase their traditions. Cultural memory, in other words, involves an ongoing process of identity construction and reconstruction motivated by collective efforts of Asian diasporas to build community solidarity. "The core meaning of any individual or group identity, namely, a sense of sameness over time and space, is sustained by remembering" (Gillis 1994, 3). It is obvious that the act of remembering is crucial for Asian diasporas to revitalize the flow of their traditions and to redefine the meaning of their cultural identities within their current social contexts.

"It is an inescapable fact about human existence that we are made of our memories: *we are what we remember ourselves to be*," as Casey so well expresses it (2000, 290). The act of remembering suggests a backward looking perspective; and in her poem "I Remember" collected in *Monsoon History*, Shirley Lim emphasizes the importance of "backward glance":

> I remember clearly child and sea.
> With time, both have grown surer.
> When, once, listening to water,
> She thought to remember the sea,
> Precise to smell, the grain
> Of shore and gathering wave,
> Mind worked furious with the grave
> Attempt. All senses strained
> To hold steady the blue motion
> Looked at. (1994, 35)

As Lim's poem suggests, memory penetrates through the fabrics of the speaker's life and makes a way into all her senses about the "sea" of her childhood. The speaker's effort "to remember the sea" indicates her "attempt" to understand herself. It is obviously impossible to arrive at an understanding of one's self without the knowledge derived from memory of the past experience. In light of this, it is no wonder that Asian diaspora poets, like Shirley Lim, express a kind of eagerness to get access to the deepest layers of memories for stored cultural values and traditions. Memory, in other words, provides Asian diaspora poets with a storage and retrieval device in which the past is remembered, re-experienced and delivered to the present. As Lim writes in another poem "Father in China":

> My father from Malaysia
> stands under a tree in China
> fifteen years ago. A lichee tree
> in Canton's People's Park. Mr. Wer
> who is also at the Clinic
> takes the picture with slightly
> shaking hands. It is a frugal picture,
> black and white, two inches by
> two inches, sent across two oceans,
> creased by crazy white lines like
> a cracked egg, although for fifteen years
> I have preserved it in plastic
> between student visas, in a succession

of wallets, between check book
and dollar notes. . . . (1998, 19)

This "frugal picture" "sent across two oceans" contains profound meanings for the speaker's memory of the past. Memory, in this regard, provides a ground for Asian diasporas to develop a sense of affinity with their traditions; and their identities are expressed by their relations to the past. According to Stuart Hall, the past "is not only a position from which to speak, but it is also an absolutely necessary resource in what one has to say" (1989, 19).

In Asian diaspora poetry, a "frugal picture" may serve as a condensed cultural image that carries collective memories and connotations for Asian diasporas. The image of "picture bride," for example, has been encoded with unusual significance for Japanese and other Asian diaspora communities. A picture bride is a woman who accepts an arranged marriage through viewing a man's picture. In the early years of Asian immigration, arranged marriage was one of the affordable and convenient ways to get married for Asian diasporas. The man usually had to toil and moil for a number of years before he could save enough money to cover his bride's transportation and living expenses in the United States. David Mura's poem "Issei: Song of the First Years in America," for instance, portrays a young girl from a small village in Japan, who comes to California to marry a Japanese diaspora farmer.

Our hair in chignons, we crowd down the planks,
our legs still wobbly from weeks at sea.
I do not expect him to be
handsome as the photo
but this is not even the same man.
The wind blows salt spray in my eyes.
Behind me I hear Keiko's muffled sobs,
the awkward greetings of a couple
who will spend half a century together.
I stare at his face. I bow.
That night it is over so quickly,
for days after, when I walk,
I feel this pebble in my shoe.
He says I must stop
eating like a sumo, must give him
a son, must clean, cook, sew—No, I think,
that is the other man, the snake that vanished
in the river in my dream, the owl

who hoots each night in the grove beyond
the rows of tomatoes and beans.
As crickets skim their cries across the night,
I squeeze a scarf between my teeth, slide
my hands open like the branches of a cedar.
Who is it who hacks here? Is this
what a baby hears inside, a howling,
a throbbing almost like love? (1995, 15)

What Mura shows here is not merely the story of a picture bride, but rather an alternative perspective on the vivid workings of her memory. The poem inscribes a condensed cultural image that represents the memories of a significant moment in the history of Japanese diaspora in America—a moment of disillusionment with the golden mountain dream.

The yearning to remember their past and the efforts to articulate their memories have entailed an ongoing process of identity recovery and construction. Memory, in other words, has played a significant role in developing identity formation, self-determination and cultural consciousness among members of Asian diaspora communities. "They need to honor the hidden histories from which they come," as Hall observes; "They need to understand and revalue the traditions and inheritances of cultural expression and creativity" (1989, 19). For this reason, memory occupies a significant place within critical discourses on culture and difference, since cultural consciousness is based on collective and individual memories of historical events, traditions and community life. At the same time, however, memory mediates between the dynamic tension of cultural preservation and cultural change, because memory as a cultural expression is by no means static or absolute. For Asian diasporas, memory is activated and produced through constant negotiations between different social, political and historical forces. Memory, in other words, incorporates the complex forces that have figured in Asian diasporas' cultural and material struggles for survival. In his well-known poem "Memory," Lawson Fusao Inada writes:

Memory is an old Mexican woman
sweeping her yard with a broom.
She has grown even smaller now,
residing at that vanishing point
decades after one dies,
but at some times, given
the right conditions—

an ordinary dream, or practically
anything in particular—
she absolutely looms,
assuming the stature
she had in the neighborhood.
. . .

Memory had been there forever.
We settled in around her;
we brought the electricity
of blues and baptized gospel,
ancient adaptations of icons,
spices, teas, fireworks, trestles,
newly acquired techniques
of conflict and healing, common
concepts of collective survival . . .

Memory was there all the while.
Her house, her shed, her skin,
were all the same—weathered—
and she didn't do anything, especially,
except hum as she moved;
Memory, in essence, was unmemorable.

Yet, ask any of us who have long since left,
who have all but forgotten that adulterated place
paved over and parceled out by the powers that be,
and what we remember, without even choosing to,
is an old woman humming, sweeping, smoothing her yard: Memory.
(1993, 50–51)

One's sense of self such as cultural or ethnic identity is actually situated in a process of searching for what one remembers in the "adulterated place" between the past and the present. The personification of memory as well as other images in the poem suggests that memory exists in and for the "common concepts of collective survival." Memory is not fixed or static but "weathered" as time flies; and therefore, we have to constantly refresh our memory of the past, just as the "old Mexican woman" is continuously "sweeping" and "smoothing her yard."

While Inada makes specific references to Mexico, a country of rich cultural memories, the poetic image that he creates, in general, has broad symbolic implications, which reveal Asian diaspora's understanding of memory. Constantly sweeping the yard of memory is essentially important for Asian diasporas, since it is an effective way to struggle against historical amnesia. What they regard as their Asian cultural heritages, in fact, is virtually absent from North American societies. As a result, they have to rely on memory as a means to re-store or re-story their fading past and to rebuild connections with their cultural traditions. One of the central themes in Asian diaspora poetry is the rehabilitation of memory as a vital part of their identity articulation. As Hall points out, almost all current arguments and debates about identity actually have roots that extend far back in time: "the relation that peoples of the world now have to their own past is, of course, part of the discovery of their own ethnicity" (1989, 19). Asian diaspora poetry provides a significant space for Asian diaspora communities to preserve their symbolic repertoires and cultural consciousness. Memory, in this sense, becomes an effective strategy for them to reinforce their original traditions and to strengthen their cultural cohesion. In his poem "Mnemonic," Li-Young Lee writes:

> I was tired. So I lay down.
> My lids grew heavy. So I slept.
> Slender memory, stay with me.
>
> I was cold once. So my father took off his blue sweater.
> He wrapped me in it, and I never gave it back.
> It was the sweater he wore to America,
> this one, which I've grown into, whose sleeves are too long,
> whose elbows have thinned, who outlives its rightful owner.
> Flamboyant blue in daylight, poor blue by daylight,
> It is black in the folds.
> . . .
> The earth is flat. Those who fall of don't return.
> The earth is round. All things reveal themselves to me only
> gradually.
>
> I won't last. Memory is sweet.
> Even when it's painful, memory is sweet. (1986, 66)

After he immigrated to the United States, Lee's relationship to his father has taken on increasingly symbolic meanings and, in a sense, it becomes a realm of memory for his understanding of the past and his tradition. In the course of his recollection, all things "reveal" themselves to him gradually, helping him revitalize his relation to the father(land). For him, the memory of his deceased father and of the values that his father represents is "sweet," even "when it's painful." This poem, so to speak, evokes not only a deep feeling of love, but also a strong sense of reviving an affectionate dialogue with a tradition. With all its symbolic implications, the father's "sweater" serves as an image for the speaker's memory of father-tradition that is persistently surviving and changing in new contexts.

In an interview, Lee mentions that his poems contain elements of both personal and impersonal connotations: "The word *father* itself," for example, "has personal connotations, yet, when I say the word, I can't help but hear impersonal connotations. All my work has been a struggle with the personal and the impersonal" (2000, 276). His memory of his father has gone beyond the boundary of individual memory to take on intersubjective dimensions. The speaker's own mental process of remembering is transformed into a collective mediation between historical and nonhistorical discourses. As Lee says, "I'm a historical being and yet an entirely nonhistorical being"; he wanted his poetry "to have that simultaneity of both the historical and the nonhistorical" (2000, 275). In comparison with history, memory is obviously nonhistorical or ahistorical. As Peter Novick points out, "Historical consciousness, by its nature, focuses on the *historicity* of events—that they took place then and not now, that they grew out of circumstances different from those that now obtain. Memory, by contrast, has no sense of the passage of time; it denies the 'pastness' of its objects and insists on their continuing presence" (1988, 4). The "continuing presence" is characteristic of Asian diaspora writings about memories which provide a vehicle to bear their cultural origin, agency and continuity. As Russell Leong says with reference to his poetic volume *The Country of Dreams and Dust*, "I wanted to show the juxtapositions between larger historical moments like, say, the Opium War and a child growing up in a Chinatown barrio a century or more later and to try to find the connection" (2000, 237). Here are a few stanzas from Leong's poem:

> Deposit dreams,
> disasters, deaths, desires
> in the flume
> of History, flotsam
> which furbishes itself.
>
> Yellow River reddens my eyes.
> Boxer rebellions inflame
> the hemorrhoids of holy pimps,

soothsayers, missionaries—
up their portals and treaty ports:
        Shanghai
Ningbo
        Amoy
Canton
        Hong Kong
. . .

A century later
The East is Red;
raw ideograms ride the waves
of a Chinese revolution
stillborn, and still to come.
. . .
May the tide configure me
from the sediment
of eastern caves,
from the mud
of temples, casinos, bars,
basements and tenements. (1993, 47–49)

For Leong, memory serves as part of the traditional resources, and plays an important role in constituting meaningful cultural bearings. Leong's self-conscious efforts to recover the past and to juxtapose it with the present suggests a willed remembrance set against diverse forces of historical amnesia, which has been intensified by the spatial and social dislocation of diaspora.

Although he has utilized plenty of historical materials in his poetic works, Leong says that his poetry is not "a reconstruction of history"; "The grand sweep of history is for traditional historians, and that presupposes that history is linear. . . . But many times, when you're just living life, you're not sure of its end point, or its beginning, or its middle" (2000, 237). In comparison with history, memory enjoys more freedom as a powerful connecting and perpetuating force in the lives of Asian diasporas. The act of remembering, therefore, is the best way of developing cultural traditions for Asian diasporas who possess no power to control mainstream history. Moreover, unlike history, remembering means reliving, since it is an emotive experience that entails the involvement of active agency. Remembering, therefore, is the action of memory that implicates a process of performance and involvement. Most importantly, the act of remembering, in Casey's words, is "intentional": "In this experience act-forms and object modes actively collaborate with each other—especially on those occasions when we are inclined to say that we have had a particularly rich or rewarding time in remembering something" (2000, 64). When reading Asian diaspora poetry, we note that the act of remembering itself is often considered as a rewarding and gratifying experience. As Li-Young Lee writes in his poem "The Gift":

> To pull the metal splinter from my palm
> my father recited a story in a low voice.
> I watched his lovely face and not the blade.
> Before the story ended, he'd removed
> the iron sliver I thought I'd die from.
>
> I can't remember the tale,
> but hear his voice still, a well
> of dark water, a prayer.
> And I recall his hands,
> two measures of tenderness
> he laid against my face
> the flames of discipline
> he raised above my head. (1986, 15)

As Lee describes in his poem, remembering is closely associated with a deep experience of vision—the sight and insight. In other words, the insight goes beneath the surface and penetrates the hidden strata of sight. The act of remembrance makes the hidden visible and brings it to light. The poet's recollection develops new principles of intelligibility whereby he is able to understand the unusual relationship between his father's "two measures of tenderness" and "the flames of discipline." Most importantly, the poet is now able to perceive in the course of his memory the successive layers of meanings which lie beneath the visible surface of his father's presence.

For Asian diasporas, remembering is the way to dig up and to make visible and sensible events from a buried storehouse of their cultural legacies; and it serves as a powerful connecting and perpetuating force in their lives, bridging the past to the present. To remember is to re-experience the past and to receive legacy from the older generations. As Jora Trang writes in her poem "Legacy":

> Today is a special day.
> No skipping rooftops or
> climbing trash bins today.

no tearing through the electrical attics
of this village, Little Saigon, today.

Today I will walk along the street
careful not to step on wayward cracks.
Today I will play my part, the escort,
as smaller children bump against me,
weaving in and out of foot traffic
lost in games I should be playing.

Savory smells of spice and sweet
slip trip from the shops within,
ducks red and marinated hung upside down,
touching and tasting things they sell,
with my grandmother at my side
in culture and colors, our distance hides.

She on the right, my on the left—
side by side, arm in arm, I hold
this legacy with no connection.
Words tongue tied in my mouth
twisting unfamiliar Vietnamese words
to break the ancient silence.
. . .

Whispers words I long to hold
In a world in which I held no power
Finally we touch, communicate
Seal the connection between the silences
I wait for the words
I wait for her touch. . . . (2000, 30–32)

To re-experience the past is part of the remembering experience. Re-experiencing assumes that one merges as part of the past event, and it is a way of representing the past that seems to involve no mediation at all. What Trang's poem shows is that remembering is not necessarily an intellectual effort but rather an experiential moment of communication that enables her to "touch" the past. Re-experiencing, therefore, may be a direct presentation of an event before it reaches the clear surface of consciousness. Garrett Hongo's poem "The Legend" provides a good example, with the first part emphasizing the re-experiencing and the second part the recollection of the event through his consciousness.

> In Chicago, it is snowing softly
> and a man has just done his wash for the week.
> . . .
> He is Asian, Thai or Vietnamese,
> and very skinny, dressed as one of the poor
> in rumpled suit pants and a plaid machinaw,
> dingy and too large.
> He negotiates the slick of ice
> on the sidewalk by his car,
> opens the Fairlane's back door,
> leans to place the laundry in,
> and turns, for an instant,
> toward the flurry of footsteps
> and cries of pedestrians
> as a boy—that's all he was—
> backs from the corner package store
> shooting a pistol, firing it,
> once, at the dumbfounded man
> who falls forward,
> grabbing at his chest.
> . . .
> Tonight, I read about Descartes'
> grand courage to doubt everything
> except his own miraculous existence
> and I feel so distinct
> from the wounded man lying on the concrete
> I am ashamed. (1996, 66–67)

Sometimes, the re-experiencing seems to be a powerful version of the past events unremembered, since some experiences such as trauma might be so tense that they slip off one's consciousness. In another poem entitled "O-Bon: Dance for the Dead," Hongo writes:

> I have no memories or photograph of my father
> coming home from war, thin as a caneworker,
> a splinter of flesh in his olive greens
> and khakis and spit-shined G.I. shores;

> . . .
> I have no memories of the radio that day
> or the clatter of machetes in the Filipino camp,
> the long wail of news from over the mountains,
> or the glimmerings and sheaths of fear in the village.
> . . .
> More than memory or the image of the slant of grey rain
> pounding the thatch coats and peaked hats
> of townsmen racing across the blond arch of a bridge,
> more than the past and its aches and brocade
> of tales and ritual, its dry mouth of repetition.
>
> I want the cold stone in my hand to pound the earth,
> I want the splash of cool or steaming water to wash my feet,
> I want the dead beside me when I dance, to help me
> Flesh the notes of my song, to tell me it's all right. (1996, 14–15)

"Dancing for the dead" means to relive the past. To be precise, re-experiencing is a special kind of memorial activity, which claims a "truth" truer than the truth and represents a "past" more than the past. In Hongo's words, it seems to be a memory "more than memory," which delivers more emotion than fact and more signification than knowledge. That is probably why Lawson Fusao Inada mentioned in his poem quoted earlier: "Memory, in essence, was unmemorable."

The unmemorable memory suggests a "black hole" in the memorial consciousness, and it is absent from the everyday experience. However, just because it is unremembered, the recovery of it would lead Asian diasporas to a better self-understanding. In Lawson Fusao Inada's poem "Kicking the Habit," we read:

> Late last night, I decided to
> stop using English.
> I had been using it all day—
>
> talking all day,
> listening all day,
> thinking all day,
> remembering all day,
> feeling all day,
>
> and even driving all day,

in English—

when finally I decided to
stop.

So I pulled off the main highway
onto a dark country road
and kept on going and going
until I emerged in another nation and. . . . (1997, 48)

In this poem, the speaker attempts to drive through spatial and temporal boundaries in order to enter "another nation" of his forefathers where English is no longer communicative. The poetic image of pulling off "the main highway onto a dark country road" vividly expresses the speaker's experience of a memory-nation and gives the speaker a new location from which to articulate his identity as part of the disarticulated tradition of Japanese diaspora, which has been buried deep in the crevices of historical amnesia. Through the act of memory, as Gloria Anzaldúa notes, the "dormant areas of consciousness are being activated, awakened" (1987, vii). Cultural memory is thus of deeply-rooted quality that survives the impact of historical forgetting. It is significant to note that Inada's poem gives voice to an unspoken, yet ever-present memory of cultural difference.

Memory is not always an entity of consistency or immanence, but rather a realm that multiplies connections and absorbs new meanings. In other words, memory is not static but changeable in different contexts. In Stuart Hall's words, "It is something that happens over time, that is never absolutely stable, that is subject to the play of history and the play of difference" (1989, 15). Memory, as a result, should be considered as a "becoming" that struggles to recuperate new relationships between the past and the present. The meanings of memory, moreover, are always subject to new questions and answers. In John Yau's poetry, we find such lines:

Memory's branch quivers
beneath the weight of a butterfly

How am I to know what it wants
without asking

Could it be that simple, the question
and then the answer

Why do we fall outside of these additions
or consult the zodiac surrounding us

read its rotten walls and bulb glare
Why substitute names for things

when the things name us
(our vowels and consonants)

into their sleep
one from which they will never awaken

Am I just an echo drifting back to myself
who is sitting beneath the river

drinking air
Something must have told me to say this

A rock or the memory of a rock
falling toward the shadow it once owned. (1992, 108–109)

Yau's compelling lines create fresh images of memory which could be as weak as a "branch" that "quivers beneath the weight of a butterfly" or as strong as a "rock" "falling toward the shadow it once owned." Memory, according to Yau, is self-reflexive, for the act of remembrance reflects an "awakening" process of searching for the true self beyond "the things" that "name us into their sleep."

Since memory communicates with people in various ways, some scholars try to differentiate two general modes of memory: individual memory and collective memory. In Asian diaspora poetry, however, the distinction is often blurred, since cultural memory works in an in-between space that is both individual and collective. It is a site of intersubjectivity, where Asian diasporas not only share their past but also shape each other through collective acts of individual remembrances. In Asian diaspora poetry, collective memory is often recorded through personal experience, while the speaker's personal life is transposed to a larger canvas of history. In this way, it is necessary to refer to memory's function as an agency for both individual and collective identities. This situation can be described with reference to Pierre Nora's idea of *lieux de mémoire* or "sites of memory." According to Nora, a *lieu de mémoire* refers to a material or nonmaterial entity that has become a "symbolic element of the memorial heritage." As Nora explains, *lieux de mémoire* exist where "memory crystallizes and secretes itself at a particular historical moment, a turning point where consciousness of a break with the past is bound up with the sense that memory has been torn" (1989, 7). Although Nora's idea is illuminating, the concept of *lieu de mémoire* has to be modified in our reading of Asian diaspora poetry, since the collective heritage represented by a *lieu de mémoire* does not necessarily endorse the mainstream national discourse. In a multicultural society, cultural heritages would be experienced and expressed individually and differently. *Lieux de mémoire*, so to speak, are unstable signs of the past that might be invested with different significances by different minority groups.

In Asian diaspora poetry, therefore, we may find the descriptions of various *lieux de mémoire*, which have special meanings for certain diaspora communities. These *lieux de mémoire*, which may have been disremembered by hegemonic history, represent the silent past of diaspora communities. Mitsuye Yamada's collections *Camp Notes* and *Desert Run*, for example, explore the silent past about the mistreatment of the members of Japanese diaspora community during World War II in the United States. In her poem "Block 4 Barrack 4 'Apt' C," Yamada describes her experience of living in an internment camp:

> The barbed fence
> protected us
> from wildly twisted
> sagebrush.
> Some were taken
> by old men with gnarled
> hands.
> These sinewed branches
> were rubbed and polished
> shiny with sweet and body oil. (1998, 19)

A few years later, the poet returned to the site of camp for a visit, which has become, at least for her, a special *lieu de mémoire* for the historical moment in her retrospection. The poet tells us:

> I spent 547 sulking days here
> in my own dreams
> there was not much to marvel at
> I thought

only miles of sagebrush and
lifeless sand.
. . .

I am back to claim my body
my carcass lies
between the spiny branches
of two creosote brushes
it took strangely like a small calf
left to graze and die
half of its bone are gone
after all these years

but no matter
I am satisfied
I take a dry stick
And give myself
A ritual burial. (1988, 2)

In Yamada's poems, the internment camp functions as a crucial site of memory, an important *lieu de mémoire*, whose significance, nonetheless, is never fully recounted in the master discourse of American mainstream history. This kind of remembering is realized with the awareness of the hegemonic force that underlies social and historical amnesia. "One aspect of the struggle between hegemonic culture and minorities," as Abdul JanMohamed and David Lloyd have observed, "is the recovery and mediation of cultural practices that continue to be subjected to 'institutional forgetting' which, as a form of control of one's memory and history, is one of the gravest forms of damage done to minority cultures" (1990, 6). As a counter-discourse to that of "forgetting," Asian diaspora poetry sets in motion a critical discourse that remembers and recollects the silent past, which has been ignored and forgotten by historical hegemony.

Asian diaspora poetry, therefore, embodies such an attempt to rediscover the silent past and to re-enact the cultural differences into history with their full social and symbolic intensity. In their writings, *lieux de mémoire*, as "souvenirs" of the past, may be encoded with new symbolic meanings of Asian diasporas' personal or collective experiences. In her poem "Souvenirs," Jessica Hagedorn writes:

in manila
my grandmother's eye

turned blue
before dying
n her secret was revealed
like a giggle
like a slow smile
from behind handpainted
pink ivory fans
scented with jasmine
n the virgin mary
sanctity n piety
are their names
n perez prado
has a number one hit
with "patricia"
on the radio

life is cheap

igorots on horseback
n the old women
chewing betel nut
in the palengke
selling kangkong leaves
the memory of war

it's so sweet sometimes. (2002, 27)

Manila, for Philippine diaspora in America, is a complex *lieu de mémoire.* The meanings it carries are multifaceted, as it connects many episodes of the speaker's memories ranging from her great grandmother's painful experience to the dreadful "martial law" dictated by "the president's wife." It is noticeable that memory provides Philippine diaspora community with a common ground on which they develop their sense of identity over time in relation to their shared past. Whether they love it or hate it, Manila, as a *lieu de mémoire,* is invested with the significance of representations of the cultural origin for Philippine diasporas' collective identity. What Hagedorn's poetry shows is that as a Philippine diaspora poet, she cannot escape from the memorial consciousness of her cultural origin, no matter how many years she has lived outside of Manila. As she writes in "Autobiography Part One: Manila to San Francisco":

In Asia
One dies slowly

Fanning off the heat
With a still palm leaf.
I love you. Garcia Villa
You are not the only one
Who is going to die
In the city
Wearing velvet slippers
And a patched red shirt
. . .

In America
The smell of death pervades
Among its women
In department stores . . . (2002, 7)

In the process of her remembering, the speaker tries to make sense and make comparison between Asia and America, the two sites of memory that she has experienced. Memory here suggests a movement across the borders of a country to connect different *lieux de mémoire* from Manila to San Francisco. The juxtaposition of various *lieux de mémoire* with different or opposite implications accentuates the action of memory as a border-crossing journey.

In an interview, Meena Alexander says that her growth as a diaspora writer can be described as "a journey across 'unquiet borders' that she never leaves behind. Alexander also calls these unquiet borders 'thresholds' in her writing. This permanent state of residing on the threshold highlights why she so values memory" (Tabios 1998, 197). In her poem "Indian April," Alexander describes her journey across the "unquiet borders" of memory in which the fragments of her life are mixed with various places or *lieux de mémoire* that have special symbolic meanings for her:

I was born at the Ganga's edge,
my mother wrapped me in a bleached sari,
laid me in stiff reeds, in hard water.

I tried to keep my nostrils above mud,
learnt how to use my limbs, how to float.
This earth is filled with black water,
small islands with bristling vines afford us some hold.
. . .

> Holy the cord of death, the sensual palaces
> of our feasting and excrement.
> Holy, the water of the Ganga, Hudson, Nile,
> Pamba, Mississippi, Mahanadi.
>
> Holy the lake in Central Park, bruised eye of earth,
> Mirror of heaven. (1999, 263–264)

For a poet who has traveled many places and crossed numerous borders, memory has taken on special significance as a vehicle for both retrospection and introspection in her writing. "Memory is very important to me," says Alexander; "Memory is also memory of ancestry. And it's part of the trajectory of people who migrate" (Tabios 1998, 197). Memory, so to speak, is part of the traversing discourse that has been contributing to the richness and complexity of the formation of diasporic identity. At the same time, Asian diaspora poets also express and contribute their own views to our understanding and exploration of the issue of memory from different perspectives.

In Asian diaspora poetry, the poetic reconstruction of the remembered or unremembered past indicates Asian diasporas' awareness and understanding of the complexity of memory. Their poetic works often highlight some aspects of memory that we never noted before. Let us read part of Lawson Fusao Inada's poem "Red Earth, Blue Sky, Petrified":

> Aspects of humanity, the human condition
> The purpose of uniting, Services, Respect.
> Responsible. Sufficient. Essential. Effects.
> Securely. Plainly. Numbered. Accordance.
> Kind. Personal. Substantial. Accepted.
> Given. Let us bring. Let us have.
> Friends, neighbors, colleagues, partners.
> Fields and places. Society and commerce.
> Rainbows. Freedom of choice, options.
> Spirits. Land. Dreams. Visions.
> Sand. Creek. Moon. Black. Red.
> Denver. Sacramento. Hiroshima.
> Battle. Creek. America. Planets.
> Marysville, Placerville, Watsonville.
> The blue tricycle left in the weeds.
> Bridge. Lights. Long since passed.
> Chanting, droning. Persistent, specific.

Shooting. Shouting. Shot. Missed.
Buddha. Buddhas. Down the rows, rows, rows.
Calligraphy of echoes. At Amache Gate.
Sit. Listen. Love. Sing. Concentrate.

Ancestry. Family. People of the land.
Home. The pattern of survival.
Continues. Remains. In full force.
Vineyards. Cottonfields. Deep.
South. Northern. West. Resources.
Above. Beneath. The spirit thrives. (1993, 176–7)

Inada's poem describes the strong momentum of his journey through various "aspects of humanity," "fields and places," "societies" and "histories," "ancestry and families." Supported by the connecting power of memory, his journey has transformed the universe into a "melody" that the poet emphasizes at the end of his poem: "A soft melody, over and over/Red earth, blue sky, petrified" (1993, 177). Inada's poem seems to suggest a kind of Buddhist understanding of memory, or *smrti*, which is more like a present-active contemplative vision, rather than the recall of past events. In fact, many Asian diaspora poetic works have exhibited the influence of Buddhism. For example, Russell Leong, whose collection *The Country of Dreams and Dust* was mentioned earlier, says that "'dreams and dust' is a Buddhist or Taoist term," although "non-Buddhist readers may get something out of it" (2000, 236). He adds, "in Buddhism, history, *karma*, a lot of things become transformed; there's a constant process of transformation and transmutation" (2000, 237). Both Leong and Inada acknowledge the importance of Buddhism and take meditative mindfulness as a form of memory. As Inada writes in one of his poems "In a Buddhist Forest":

Even if you're not Buddhist,
Even if you don't know
Anything about Buddhism,

Even if you're not interested
In its precepts and paths,
Even if you're anti-Buddhist,

Your Buddhist Self proceeds

Accordingly, in a Buddhist city,
In a Buddhist forest . . . (1997, 47)

In Leong's and Inada's poems, the Buddhist notion of memory provides a background for their modern meditations on the past in both spiritual and epistemological senses. The practices of mindfulness indicate a rich cultural tradition from the Orient, where memory is not always separable from the spiritual world of infinite past lives.

Buddhist notion of memory cannot be understood entirely in terms of Western rationalism, since it transcends the realms of the empirically verifiable and the rational, and touches the nerve of our spirituality. In this sense, some Asian diaspora poets move toward the subversion of our rational perceptions, elaborating on the questions of memory beyond our ordinary senses. Let us take Meena Alexander's poem "Golden Horizon" for example. This poem is subtitled "The 'Unquiet Borders' of Memory," in which memory is personified as "a ghost-woman" who is both the speaker's companion and muse:

She walks towards me whispering
Dried petals in her hair
A form of fire
But her skin
Like finest Dacca cotton
Drawn through a gold ring, spills

Over bristling water.
Something has hurt her.
Can a circlet of syllables

Summon her from the Vagai river?
She kneels by a bold stone
Cuts glyphs on its side, waves to me.

Our language is in ruins–
Vowels impossibly sharp,
Broken consonants of bone.

She has no home. (Tabios 1998, 207–208)

Memory, like the "ghost woman," is diasporic and has no home. She wanders around the world and sometimes travels to the other side of existence to reveal the intangible dimensions of life. Alexander's poem competes with the conventional understanding of memory; and it portrays vividly the poet's quest for relocating her sense of identity beyond the boundary of her empirical senses. By juxtaposing the phenomenal and spiritual worlds and by layering both rational and nonrational elements in life, Alexander's poem creates an image of a larger, eternal whole of which one's individual memory and experience are only a tiny part. The alternative perspective on memory as suggested by Alexander's poem has special significance in a broad cultural context, since among all other things the diasporic "ghost woman" signifies the speaker's cultural root—the depth and breadth of her identity.

Asian diaspora poetry recognizes multiplicity and complexity of memory; and it encourages readers to pass through the world of sensory experience and to search for full meaning of memory in the negotiations between the real and the unreal, and betwixt the ordinary and the extraordinary. The difference between Eastern and Western concepts of memory is an interesting issue. In his study of memory, Edward Casey has noted that "In China," for example, "the house opens onto the garden and is thus not a self-contained place of memory; being only part of a garden compound that is a microcosm of nature, its role in remembering is that of a vestibule and its memorial significance is quite literally marginal." By contrast, Casey points out, "In the Western world, where dwellings are so often closed off from nature, it is therefore not surprising to be told that 'the house is one of the greatest powers of integration for the thoughts, memories, and dreams of mankind'" (2000, 211). To use house and garden as metaphors, we probably can understand that the Eastern notions of memory are more open-ended than "self-contained." Memory, as represented by Asian diaspora poetry, often refers to a realm that multiplies associations and constantly absorbs new elements. In the processes of cultural dispersal and dislocation, their memory provides an important channel for Asian diasporas to associate the past with the present, the West with the East, the real with the imagined. In this respect, as Richard Terdiman remarks, "memory with its unending and uncompassable associations is the modality of culture itself" (2003, 193). For Asian diasporas, to embrace memory is to possess and repossess their cultural traditions, and the remembrance of their past forms an integral part of their affirmation of cultural identity. Here is Ha Jin's poem "To an Ancient Chinese Poet":

That night you were very drunk
You banged your *pipa* on a stone table.
The moon could not set up
the upset cups scattered around,

although it was sharpening your saber
standing on a single-log bridge.
The poems on scarps of paper were gone with the breeze.
You allowed them to fall into a river
which abounded with tadpoles and apple blossoms.

"What's the use of fame as a poet?"
you yelled at the foggy night,
"it's a silent affair a thousand years after me.
After me!" You raised your empty hand,
"Let me drink," and fell to the ground,
"Let me sleep." You were
fast asleep on the precipice.

It is a thousand years now.
Today, I put my hand into another river
whose water is clear and warm.
Tadpoles and apple blossoms
are flowing through my fingers
while the cold passion of your poems
is penetrating through my arm. (1990, 65–66)

Ha Jin's poem reverberates with the long tradition of Asian cultural sensibilities. The image of the ancient Chinese poet, as seen through the prism of memory, enables the poet to connect himself to a long literary tradition; and more importantly, it enables him to assert an identity connected with her cultural ancestry. Cultural memory, therefore, provides a wide, enriching landscape for the poet to relocate the deep dimension of his identity, and confirms his renewed attachment to his heritage which, in turn, gives him the feeling of belonging, collective awareness and self-consciousness. These awareness and consciousness, moreover, do not merely yield an insight into the past, but more importantly, suggest a vision of the future. "What is crucial to such a vision of the future," to use Homi Bhabha's words, "is the belief that we must not merely change the *narratives* of our histories, but transform our sense of what it means to live, to be, in other times and different spaces, both human and historical" (1994, 256).

Chapter Six

Against the Grain of Cultural Exoticism

The Other Question

> The "exotic" is uncannily close. Conversely, there seem no distant places left on the planet where the presence of "modern" products, media and power cannot be felt.
>
> James Clifford
>
> *The Predicament of Culture* (1988, 13)

> To imagine otherwise is not simply a matter of seeing a common object from different perspectives. Rather, it is about undoing the very notion of common objectivity itself and about recognizing the ethicopolitical implications of multiple epistemologies—theories about knowledge formation and the status and objects of knowledge—that underwrite alternative perspectives.
>
> Kandice Chuh
>
> *Imagine Otherwise* (2003, x)

The image of the "exotic" is an important aspect of cultural representation, which is usually associated with the notion of cross-cultural encounter, and implies change, transformation and appropriation of a culture in different sociopolitical and historical contexts. As a consequence of the encounter between different systems of social signification, cultural exoticization takes on special significance in the transnational space that provides common ground for conducting debates over the representation of cultural otherness. The cultural images of Oriental women, for example, have long been circulated in the West and their irresistible exotic features have obtained a symbolic order of cultural otherness. As Cathy Song describes in her poem about Kitagawa Utamaro's paintings of Japanese women:

He drew hundreds of women
in studies unfolding
like flowers from a fan.
Teahouse waitresses, actresses,
geishas, courtesans and maids.
They arranged themselves
before this quick, nimble man
whose invisible presence
one feels in these prints
is as delicate
as the skinlike paper
he used to transfer
and retain their fleeting loveliness. (37)

For many years, the exquisite images of the lovely "paper women" have traversed beyond the boundaries of their original cultural territories, acquiring fetishistic meanings under the Western gaze. "The traditional imagery of the Other," as Zhang Longxi observes, "has an aura of mystery, exotic beauty" (52). The Orient, in other words, has become a diasporic signifier, deterritorialized, translated and disseminated in the West, expressing the West's desires and interests. However, the Orient never acquires a position of "a free subject of thought." As Rey Chow notes, if the Orient were not "a free subject," then it could not itself be an "object" either, since it is "a mere 'signifier' of something further" (12). In such circumstances, cultural exoticization produces a disjunction between the signifier and the signified that causes cultural mistranslation between the East and the West. As Marilyn Chin writes:

Amerigo has his finger on the pulse of China.
He, Amerigo, is dressed profoundly punk:
Mohawk-pate, spiked dog collar, black leather thighs.
She, China, freshly hennaed and boaed, is intrigued
with the new diaspora and the sexual freedom
called *bondage*. "Isn't *bondage*, therefore,
a *kind* of freedom?" she asks, wanly. (80)

The poem, in an ironic sense, helps us perceive the internal politics of cultural exoticization and recognize the complexity associated with representation of the Other or otherness across different cultures. Since the early years of colonialism, cultural exoticization has been a common practice of Western opinion-makers. The mysterious "Oriental" of Marco Polo, the "noble savage" of Jean Jacques Rousseau and the romantic "South Sea Islanders" of Paul Gauguin are only a few examples. To a certain degree, exoticization implicates a process of cross-cultural domination, for the signification of Asian exotic cultures, according to Edward Said, suggests "a Western style for dominating, restructing, and having authority over the Orient" (3). By means of rendering the Orient into discursive constructions, Western culture "gained in strength and identity by setting itself off against the Orient as a sort of surrogate and even underground self" (3). Cultural exoticism, therefore, is permeated with Western viewpoints and ideological influences, and moreover, as Rey Chow observes, it implicates a kind of "mentalism, the tendency that treats the world as a result of ideas, which in turn are construed as the products of the human mind" (1998, xx). Referring to Jacques Derrida's reading of "the inscrutable Chinese," Chow says: "The face of the Chinese person and the face of Chinese writing thus converge in what must now be seen as a composite visual stereotype—*the-other-as-face*—that stigmatizes another culture as at once corporeally and linguistically intractable" (2002, 64-65).

The Orient became a subject of interest to the West during the Enlightenment and its appeal became increasingly widespread through the Romantic movement and the advancement of modern imperialism. The romantic fascination with the Orient, however, has the effect of superimposing Western values onto other cultures, creating an exotic picture that describes Western perspectives more than the Oriental reality. Asian diaspora poets have to deal with cross-cultural representation in a way that both subverts the practice of exoticism and challenges the dualistic mode of thinking. For them, the entities of East and West are not absolutely separate or oppositional. While the East may be a construction of the West, the opposite is just as true: the West is also a construction of the East. These complexities and contradictions are reflected in the poetic expressions of Asian diasporic writings.

Asian diaspora poetry constructs a paradoxical discourse that incorporates both the imagery of exoticism and a critical perspective that subverts the very practice of exoticization. For the poets, this mode of writing demands a considerable degree of self-reflexive control in their explorations of self-identity. Asian diaspora poetry, in other words, challenges us to rethink the practice of cultural exoticization in relation to Western ideological appropriations. As Dan Bacalzo describes in his poem:

> "I like my Asians to look like Asians,"
> a lover once told me.

> "You have a very feminine face,"
> said another.
>
> What is it they expect from me?
> What fantasy do I fulfill?
> Feminine?
> Boyish?
> Oriental? (2000, 33)

The expectation of the poet's friends described here is related to the issue of cross-cultural fantasy, which feeds on the exotic (sur)face of the Asian or the Asian diaspora. This poem, to a certain extent, expresses the poet's self-reflexive knowledge that a culture may become outlandish in one way or another when it crosses its borders into a different sociopolitical territory. In a different context, cultural differences can become so visible and glaring that they may take on some significances and meanings previously unnoticed or invisible in their original territories. Diaspora as a process of traversing the boundaries of different cultures has inevitably given rise to questions about cultural exoticization, and it has touched the sensitive nerve of an epistemological system in which the ideological appropriations still influence people's perceptions and conceptions of Asian diasporas. As Amita Vasudeva depicts:

> "Can you talk Mexican?"
> They used to ask me.
> "No, I'm not Mexican I'm Indian, and besides they speak Spanish,"
> I used to reply, waiting eagerlessly for their best
> Attempt at doing a "raindance."
> "Owwow ooh ow ow." Smacking outstretched palms to their little
> mouths and hopping around.
> "Not THAT kind of Indian—Indian from India."
> I would correct, as soon as they finished whooping.
> "Oh . . . Can you talk Indian?" (1995, 70)

The experience of encountering the "Owwow ooh ow ow" raindance points to an "exquisite truth" that lies behind the whooping show. Similar to Bacalzo's work, this poem represents a subtle self-awareness of the speaker, who is mistaken for the Other. The ironic power of this poem comes from the speaker's ability to imagine how others imagine her as the Other. In American society, the image of Asian diasporic subjects has been wittingly or unwittingly constituted as the embodiment of the exotic Other; and the pervasive exoticism has forced the speaker into being someone she is not. Although any stranger can be exotic to someone else, systematic exoticization is achieved only by the dominant culture that has the power and privilege to promote its own values and judgments as "universal."

Against the topos of various Western representations of the Other, Asian diaspora poets have to cope with the task of re-presenting the "other" dimension of their identity in a way that inscribes their own reflections on themselves. Since Western cultural exoticism has developed a global epistemological frame in which cultural identity is often a preconditioned version that expresses Western perspectives, Asian diaspora poets must rewrite and represent themselves in new ways; and these self-representations disrupt the existing paradigm of interpretation and power relations. The practice of self-reflexivity that we find in Asian diaspora poetry not only exposes the binary structure of cultural or racial exoticism but also converts this structure into a new mode of representation that subverts the dominant ideology in American society. Asian diaspora poets, therefore, have developed their self-representations in a manner that not only deconstructs the myth of the Other, but also breaks the very ideological framework of epistemology that underwrites cultural exoticism. As Merle Woo writes in "Yellow Woman Speaks,"

> And I will expose the lies and ridicule
> the impotence of those who have called us
> chink
> yellow-livered
> slanted cunts
> exotic
> in order to abuse and exploit us.
> And I will destroy them. (1991, 216)

Through reimagining her identity, Woo is able to "expose the lies" of ideological stereotypes. At the same time, the poet successfully works out a kind of rewriting or reinstatement of her identity against Western preconceptions about the Other. Woo's poem can be described as a self-reflexive representation that holds up to ridicule racial exoticization. In confronting Western preconceptions of stereotyped Oriental women, Asian diaspora poets attempt to rewrite their cultural images beyond existing stereotypes. As Diane Mei Lin Mark put it in her poem,

Suzie Wong
doesn't live here anymore
yeah, and
Madame Butterfly
And the geisha ladies have all gone
. . .
no one here
but ourselves
        stepping on,
without downcast eyes,
without calculating dragon power,
without tight red cheongsams
  embroidered with peonies
without the
silence
that you've come to
know so well
and we
to feel so alien with (1991, 182)

Mark's poem represents new cultural images that subvert and de-exoticize the established stereotypes of Oriental women. There is no more "Suzie Wong" or China doll; and the meek "Madame Butterfly" and subservient "geisha ladies" have all gone. What we witness here are new figures of Asian diaspora women "without downcast eyes" and "without tight red cheongsams." This subversive discourse urges the reader to scrutinize the image of the Other beneath its exotic (sur)face.

The scrutiny, in Rey Chow's words, incorporates a mode of cross-cultural resistance "against the active imposition on the relations between West and non-West of an old epistemological hierarchy" (1995, 27). Historically, this "epistemological hierarchy" was established by Western anthropologists who, while studying non-Western cultures, imposed consciously or unconsciously a Western conceptual system upon "the primitive." What the earlier anthropologists didn't predict is that "the primitive" today has outgrown the old concepts and assumptions that were based on their limited understanding of cultural differences. As Zhang Longxi points out, "it would be wrong to forget that the Other has its own voice and can assert its own truth against various misconceptions" (1998, 48). The poetic works by Asian diaspora writers actually embody their search for new voices to express their self-understanding outside of the confines of Western epistemological hierarchy. In Shirley Lim's words,

> Poetry
> asks understanding.
> Its sign, compression,
> acknowledges to conceal:
> widening centric motions
> of a swimming floundering,
> striking out for shore
> or horizon, a sign
> insistent on survival,
> breaking the bottomless
> surface of ocean. (1994, 76)

Poetry writing, for Asian diasporas, is an act of exploration that breaks the "bottomless surface of ocean" for a new "shore" of knowledge. It is also a practice that aims at representing the "Oriental cultures" that people have taken for granted, and "asks for understanding" of new meanings that have been concealed by layers of ideological beliefs. Asian diaspora poetry, therefore, characterizes an interrogative mode of writing that investigates the complicated system of cultural exoticism by means of both presenting and questioning what it presents simultaneously. As a result, Asian diaspora poets are acquiring a distinctive presence in their attempt to analyze their own cultural traditions through cross-cultural negotiation with the appropriations and exoticizations of mainstream ideology.

In the process of cross-cultural negotiation and in challenging Western assumptions, Asian diaspora poets raise searching questions: What is the appropriate discourse for representing "otherness" in today's world? To what extent are Asian diasporic subjects able to represent a distinct cultural identity from that of the Other? These questions, as Homi Bhabha notes, challenge "any essentialist claims for the inherent authenticity or purity of cultures which, when inscribed in the naturalistic sign of symbolic consciousness frequently become political arguments for the hierarchy and ascendancy of powerful cultures" (1995, 58). What Asian diaspora poetry challenges is precisely the cultural hierarchy; it advocates a new turn in the process of cross-cultural negotiation as the poets begin to represent themselves in contrast to various kinds of cultural subalternization. In this sense, Asian diaspora poetry suggests the prospect of addressing a more profound cross-cultural negotiation which people are currently experiencing. The challenge to cultural hierarchy which Asian diaspora poetry makes constitutes a new horizon of that cultural politics whereby traditionally marginalized voices have emerged to question the Western privilege and hegemonic power in cultural domination. Shirley Lim writes in her poem "I Defy You":

I defy you Wallace Stevens
to prove 'the exquisite truth.'
Your thirteen blackbirds rolled in one
continuous seamless world
bob in and out of my world
as do the black men and women
in Durban who skitter
on my tv screen. There is something else
than mere vision, mere imagination,
fat man of language. Something
than words and quiet time and cold mind,
although you have emptied your pockets
and peeked over the horizon of our desires
and turned back preferring your onanistic treasures.
The young Cambodian whose father drowned
in monsoon ocean knows
his sister's raped eyes are truth;
the hungry and dead are his 'exquisite truth,'
and you an American fiction. (1994, 93)

The representation of the "young Cambodian" and "his sister's raped eyes" in contrast to Stevens's exotic imagery of "blackbirds rolled in one continuous seamless world" juxtaposes the "hard" and "exquisite" truth. It is not surprising, therefore, that in the process of global diaspora Asian diasporic subjects are asserting strong voices. Such cultural self-representation, in Lawrence Venuti's words, should be regarded as "a strategic cultural intervention in the current state of world affairs, pitched against the hegemonic English-state nations and the unequal cultural exchanges in which they engage their global others" (1995, 20). Obviously, self-representation does not aim at preserving a fixed, pre-translated identity; but rather it destabilizes and challenges the epistemology that underwrites the "exquisite truth" of cultural exoticism. "At such a historic juncture," as Wolfgang Iser notes, "a cross-cultural discourse begins to emerge," which is "motivated by the need to cope with a crisis that can no longer be alleviated by the mere assimilation or appropriation of other cultures" (1996, 248). This new cross-cultural discourse inscribes changes and transformations of the Other and activated fresh interactions between different cultures.

As a result of the global flows of cultural diaspora, the location of the Other has been changed and is no longer confined to the remote areas far away from the metropolitan centers. Westerners nowadays no longer need to go abroad to meet the exotic Orient, since, as Chandra Mohanty points out, the Orient is found in New York, Los Angeles, Paris, London and Berlin (1991, 4). The Other next door or down the street raises further questions for cross-cultural negotiations inside the so-called multicultural societies of North America. As James Clifford observes, in the age of diaspora, "the 'exotic' is uncannily close. Conversely, there seem no distant places left on the planet where the presence of 'modern' products, media and power cannot be felt" (1988, 13). In Saleem Peeradina's poem, we read:

> The other is a neighborhood beyond
> your skin's barbed wire fence; an uninvited
> guest from a future age who could have been
> your rescuer before your memory betrayed
> his origins. (1995, 60)

In Asian diaspora poetry, the issue of the Other in the neighborhood is often foregrounded with the discussion of "multiculturalism" which, nevertheless, does not help Asian diasporic subjects escape from the confining system of exoticization. On the contrary, they are "nurtured" to stay in the image of the exotic for the purpose of "multiculturalism." As Thelma Seto shows in "Living in the Margins":

> How to convince you people
> we want you here, want not
> to exclude you?
> You are exotic, romantic.
> You just need nurturing.
>
> We're here to promote our special project,
> the one that won the grant money
> . . .
> We know English is your mother tongue,
> your only language, the one your parents adopted,
> relinquishing their native tongue
> to survive among us.
>
> Such a loss. We've tried to make it up to you
> by learning your parents' language,
> converting to Zen Buddhism,
> which we'd love to teach you,

living a life of chaste
trans-continental
poverty,
translating your classical writers
so you can read them.
Maybe learning haiku.
You needn't submit haiku,
though it would be a nice touch.
We wrote "multi-cultural" in our grant proposal.
That's why we got the money. (1995, 161–162)

Seto's sarcastic poem describes how Asian diasporic subjects have become an exotic "object" of investigation for multicultural projects. The so-called "multiculturalism" seems to be a kind of cultural intervention that implicates the deprivation of Asian voices in the representation of Asian cultures. It urges that members of Asian diaspora communities be assimilated into mainstream American culture, yet also asks them to maintain the exotic "outward show" of Asian customs as adornments to sustain the myth of a diverse society, but without altering the cultural hierarchy, racial marginalization and political domination.

Asian diaspora poetry, in a sense, does not turn away from "well-intentioned" multiculturalism; instead it confronts it and includes it in a cross-cultural negotiational process, a two-way interaction which responds to, resists and so progressively transforms cultural exoticization. The self-conscious play with the stereotyped "outward show" as a "mask," which such negotiation exhibits, points to a paradoxical practice of cultural self-portrayal whereby Asian diaspora poets represent themselves as a new, self-assured "Other." Mitsuye Yamada writes:

Over my mask
is your mask
of me
an Asian woman
grateful
gentle
in the pupils of your eyes
as I gestures with each
new play of
light
and shadow

> this mask be
> comes you. (1988, 87)

What we find in the play of double mask is a mutual mirroring effect. When the Other represents herself in the mirror, it actually pulls apart the mask/image of the Other through the mirror, initiating a new relationship between the self and the Other. The Other or, to be exact, the self-reflexive Other, is the beginning, but not the ending of the "epic journey" towards a full understanding of the self. As Peeradina asserts,

> The other is a new taste, an echo
> from a distant shore, any place you have
> not been before, a country that insists on
> occupying the map, an unforeseen epic
> journey. (1995, 59–60)

Owing to their new awareness of racial, national and cultural differences intensified by their diasporic experience, Asian diasporas inevitably feel that they have been otherized in a new society. The experience of being the Other threatens their sense of identity as a fixed, pure and closed structure that has been uprooted from its original cultural territory. Meanwhile, however, this experience also pushes them into the search for a new sense of self in relation to the image of the Other, since after relocating themselves in America, Asian diasporas must look at themselves in new contexts formed by different political and cultural forces. As Ha Jin describes in his poem "In New York City," his diasporic experience has translated him into "another man"—a living image of the Other, which paradoxically corroborates his sense of the self as a wandering stranger in a metropolitan center.

> In the golden rain
> I plod along Madison Avenue,
> loaded with words.
> They are from a page
> that shows the insignificance
> of a person to a tribe,
> just as a hive keeps thriving
> while a bee is lost.
>
> On my back the words
> are gnawing and gnawing

till they enter into my bones—
I become another man,
alone, wandering,
no longer dreaming of luck
or meeting a friend. (1996, 62)

Diaspora, which opens up new spaces for negotiation between the self and the Other, creates radical effects of dislocation in identity articulation. The speaker in the poem searches for accurate words to express his experience of dislocation in the Big Apple. His life in diaspora has been translated and transformed into a new system of social and cultural signification that gives the diaspora the "other" position to re-view and to rearticulate himself.

The negotiation between the self and the Other suggests a critical consciousness that underscores an ironic tension in the mirroring process of self-portrayal as the Other within different cultural formations. In John Yau's words, it is an interactive strategy of looking at oneself as the Other in an attempt to redefine one's identity, and it is an attempt to speak from the "other" side of the self:

"When I am *in* my painting, I'm not aware of what I'm doing"
when aware of what I am in my painting, I'm not aware
when I am my painting, I'm not aware of what I am
when what, what when, what of, when in, I'm not painting my I
when painting, I am I what I'm doing, not doing what I am
when doing what I am, I'm not in my painting,
when I am of my painting, I'm not aware of when, of what
of what, when, my, I, painting, in painting
when of, of what, in when, in what, painting
not aware, not in, not of, not doing, I'm in my I
in my am, not am in my, not of when I am, of what
painting "what" when I am, of when I am, doing, painting.
when painting, I'm not doing. I am in my doing. I am painting.
(2002, 12)

As Yau's idiosyncratic poem shows, in order to understand one's "self," one must take a second view from "the other" side. Self-portrayal or self-painting must be done from an alternative angle to that of one's self. The self, in other words, is actually a product of this inside-outside practice of performance—as Yau says, "I'm not doing. I am in my doing. I am painting." This experience reminds us of what Jacques Derrida calls "the phenomenon of hearing-oneself-speak in order to mean-to-say" (1998, 25). Anyone who wants to produce a self-portrait must take a psycho-intellectual detour in order to acquire an "other-wise" vision outside the boundary of one's self. Self-representation, to a certain extent, seems to be a process of self-alienation—The self asserts itself under its own watchful eyes. In Derrida's opinion, "This abiding alienation appears, like lack, to be constitutive. But it is neither a lack nor an alienation: it lacks nothing that precedes or follows it, it alienates no ipseity, no property and no self that has ever been able to represent its watchful eye" (1998, 25).

The acknowledgement of the alienating "watchful eye" is associated with the "other" sensitivity that enables one to understand simultaneously two or more cultural viewpoints. As Janice Raymond observes, this ability might be called "two sights seeing" (1986, 205). Orientalist discourse, however, by claiming the Western cultural values as "human and universal," negates any other forms of cultural perception and insight. To a certain extent, Asian diaspora poets can be seen as embodying the self-conscious attempt to represent themselves in "two sights," and the practice of "two sights seeing" leads to a better understanding of the self as dialogic, which cannot be appropriated by means of monovision. Yau's poem requires us to recognize and appreciate the value of "two sights" within their expressions of the self. The "mark of splitting" indicates the dialogic nature of diasporic identity. Since diasporic identity is defined across cultural and national differences, the noticeable otherness has become an inevitable dialogic element of inheritance. Moreover, the inherited elements may give rise to a process of identity reformation in which foreignness and strangeness are translated into measures capable of reinventing the self. As David Woo's poem shows:

The habit of staring
at a stranger's profile
in the teeming deli
or off-hour café
the habit of looking away,
tilting your face into your *Times*,
grazing the squeaky white rim
of your espresso cup,
looking away from the face that looks back
with interest or disdain or suspicion,
in infinite gradations,
like the faces of those who shed

their strangeness and became your friends—
the face of Anna, who smiled serenely,
or Yang Ping, who furrowed his brow,
or Martin, who grimaced—
the habit of seeing in a stranger's
accidental gesture
or deliberate expression,
the finger patting the side of the jaw,
the pull, tiny, discreet,
of an earlobe or disheveled collar,
even the clumsy wink,
the leer, the rapacious grin,
the habit of seeing in any attitude
what Baudelaire called
the glance that brought him back to life,
played over and over again
in the faces of others,
reviving you, resuscitating you,
propelling you back into yourself
or, better yet, out of yourself—
(1993, 287)

The interesting form of this poem implicates a relationship of "two sights" between the self and the Other, and between different systems of cultural signification, activating the modes of cultural interaction that accommodate new strategies for identity formation by including otherness in self-representation. To represent one's self, one must stay out of the boundary of the self and look at the self as the Other. The complicated relationship between the self and the Other is well expounded by Zhang Longxi in his reading of Wu Xiaoming: "Wu is quite right to maintain that 'it is possible to define the self only through the Other. The myth of the self can be generated only by forgetting or suppressing the conditions that make the self possible as self, by forgetting or suppressing the fact that the self is also an Other to the Other" (1998, 145). In a sense, Asian diaspora poetry confronts the split between the self and the Other with a new cultural representation that produces a realm of otherness that the self-conscious Other must reclaim.

Asian diaspora poetry hence inscribes a mode of self-reflexivity that invokes a counter-perspective to Western cultural exoticism. In other words, Asian diaspora poets have enacted a self-reflexive role in their attempts to reimagine their cultural identity, not as the "inscrutable" Other, but as "presumptuous" speakers who have confident voices. As Nellie Wong says,

> We never asked to be mysterious.
> We never asked to be inscrutable.
> Still untold stories, untold histories.
> Still the unknown unknown.
> Retrieve burnt letters, receipts, bills,
> anything written, anything spoken?
> Our dreams in bones and ashes?
> To be seen and heard.
> To be known but not merely by our many names.
> Being presumptuous I speak for myself.
> Others who remain silent own their own tongues. (2003, 183)

The desire to assert their own voices and to speak for themselves has formed new generations of the Other who are no longer silent, mysterious or inscrutable, but capable of self-analysis, self-representation in Western style and self-translation in English. Most importantly, they know how to use exotic terms to counter exoticism. These poets stand between two cultural worlds mastering both with equal competence, but in order for their critique of Western prejudice to be understood, they have to challenge exoticist *mentalité* on its own grounds by using the same language and concepts. For Asian diaspora poets, the issue of language is closely related to their cultural difference and life experience. "Alienation institutes every language as a language of the other," as Derrida points out; "The language called maternal is never purely natural, nor proper, nor inhabitable. . . . There is no possible habitat without the difference of this exile and this nostalgia" (1998, 58). The situation that Derrida describes is particularly intensified in the case of Asian diaspora. As Marilyn Chin writes in her poem "The Colonial Language Is English":

> Heaven manifests its duality
> My consciousness on earth is twofold
> My parents speak with two tongues
> My mother's tongue is Toisan
> My father's tongue is Cantonese
> The colonial language is English
> . . .

The Tao of which we speak is not the eternal Tao
The name that we utter is not the eternal name
My mother is me, my father is thee
As we drown in the seepage of Sutter Mill. (2002, 20–21)

Chin's poem highlights a paradoxical situation of "language of the other." English, as the speaker tells us, is the other language that is not "natural, nor proper, nor inhabitable," since it inscribes Eurocentric consciousness. For Asian diaspora poets, to write themselves in English is to develop new identities in a language that is not their own. By bringing new consciousness into English, their choice of language carries special significance in their poetic imagination. Ha Jin writes,

I know my cries in this alphabet
will compound my "crimes" and take me further away
from you, my dearest friend. But I have to write
and have to choose between being a good citizen
or a good writer. For the Chinese,
nobility lies in claiming both.
This means to sacrifice one's life
for the integrity of one's words.
Sacrifice, oh sacrifice, it will only end
in the truncation of the meaningful work
that might eventually bring honor to our race. (1996, 66)

Exiled from his original language—Chinese, Ha Jin tries to rewrite himself in English. In this "alphabetic" tongue, he searches for "the integrity" of his words without "the truncation of meaningful work." Although English might be the first language for many Asian diaspora poets, they still experience a process of cultural retuning. Their writings often express a critical consciousness that reflects their individual use of English which connects to their cultural sensibilities. In the land of English, they are at once the masters and the interlopers.

By mastering English, Asian diaspora poets are able to make their voices heard in the West, breaking the silence produced by Western linguistic and cultural domination. Their writing resists hegemonic subalternization and, furthermore, challenges the power relations that lie behind the production of exotic images, stereotypes and constructions. In the following poem, Lê Thi Diem Thúy attempts "to tear apart the silence" and to tell her audience that Vietnamese diasporic subjects are much more complex than Western stereotypes suggest:

I tell you all this
to tear apart the silence
of our days and nights here

I tell you all this
to fill the void of absence
in our history here

we are fragmented shards
blown here by a war no one wants to remember

in a foreign land
with an achingly familiar wound
our survival is dependent upon
never forgetting that Vietnam is not
a word
a world
a love
a family
a fear
to bury
. . .
but a piece
of
us,
sister
and
we are
so much

more (2000, 225–226)

The statement that "we are so much more" is a call for representation and reinterpretation of their cultural identities. Asian diaspora poetry, in this sense, encourages reflections and thoughts about national histories and traditions, working against exoticist discourses. In Christian Langworthy's poem "How I Could Interpret the Events of my Youth," the speaker's retelling of his life in Vietnam is by no means intended for an exotic story about the tropical South China Sea:

> Because I was a newly adopted
> child from another country,
> (a prostitute's son in a Vietnamese
> city bristling with rifles
> and as a result of my mother's truancy
> from motherhood I was given
> to nuns and locked within the confines
> of missionary walls)
> I crossed the perilous South China Sea
> and Pacific in three days
> (barely surviving anti-aircraft fire)
> aboard an eight prop-engine plane.
> I came to this country
> to a nine-inch carpet of snow
> and a sure welcome by strangers
> engaged with the possibilities of parenthood.
> . . .
>
> As the years of my second life progressed,
> my adopted parents tried so to be
> a good father and mother and to the cinema
> we went, and I saw the children's epics:
> Snow White and the Seven Dwarves
> and Sleeping Beauty; at home my mother read
> fairy tales to me, tales like Rumpelstiltskin,
> and I learned
> the fairy beauty of the wicked witch,
> the castle besieged by thorns,
> the terror of the kidnapped son.
> I could have told them I'd seen these tales
> before, but I was too young to know the difference. (2000, 60–61)

By comparing his previous life in Vietnam with his new life in America, the speaker searches through historical and cultural particulars to find a new interpretation of the events of his youth. There are no descriptions of lush landscapes or sensual waters; instead, phrases like "the perilous South

China Sea," "anti-aircraft fire," "the confines of missionary walls" and "the castle besieged by thorns" dispel fantasies about the Orient.

The anti-exotic stance in Asian diaspora poetry might be understood with reference to what Mary Pratt calls "autoethnography." By autoethnography, Pratt means "instances in which colonized subjects undertake to represent themselves in ways that *engage with* the colonizer's own terms." "If ethnographic texts are a means by which Europeans represent to themselves their (usually subjugated) others," Pratt says, "autoethnographic texts are those the others construct in response to or in dialogue with those metropolitan representations" (1992, 7). In the process of cross-cultural negotiation, Asian diaspora poets develop an intercultural dialogue between the East and the West. However, their self-representation is more than autoethnography, for their intercultural dialogue between East and West, which makes Asian diasporas more aware of their "otherness" in American society, turns ethnographic exoticism upside down. In some of their poems, Asian diaspora poets may consciously include exotic descriptions and imageries of themselves, but their autoexoticism both acknowledges and challenges Western ideological viewpoints. In Fay Chiang's poems, for example, the autoethnographic account of the life of Asian diasporas in the United States is delivered in a critical perspective that confronts the mainstream ideology in American society:

mahjong and dice on the tables upstairs
        the noise confusion of trucks and cars and calls and
                                children and cars and dogs and
traffic stream of people
        traffic upstream downstream
and children and women and men and
        people and people locked in the safety
                feeling trapped
                in crumbling tenements
slipping/sliding down the
                mountain of gold

. . .

        I studied asians in america
        I demonstrated against the war in Indochina
                        and shouted chilai, kaibo, makibaka
        don't forget

all the nights we wrote newsletters and flyers
the times we leafleted and petitioned
for community issues

. . .

I want to be mobile and hitching cross country
through europe and africa
the great escape
before the blue collar job
where I'm living at least on the poverty level
I want a piece of the golden mountain
a piece of the big apple pie-in-the-sky
so please,
don't tell me it's all a lie. (1999, 327–329)

In Chiang's poem, the outlandish customs of "mahjong and dice" and the mention of "chilai, kaibo, makibaka" do not evoke any alluring fantasies that were conventionally associated with the notion of the exotic. Autoethnographic depiction, in this case, has been transformed into an anti-exotic discourse that is subversive and resistant against the "lie" hidden behind the myth of the American dream created by the mainstream ideology.

Moreover, Asian diaspora poetry often involves defamiliarization as Asian diaspora poets take an estranged look at their own original cultures in a contradictory mode of double writing. Self-exoticization is sometimes adopted as a writing strategy in order to otherize and defamiliarize the poet's own cultural tradition, subjecting it to detached examination. This contradictory discourse, in Scott Nygren's words, "foregrounds the necessary distorting process of the Imaginary or Other as a means by which difference can be conceived" (1993, 182). What these poems suggest, beneath the exotic surface, is cultural transposition between different signifying systems, which reifies cultural referents to new signifieds. Cultural transposition recontextualizes their own cultural traditions in relation to their diasporic experience and, moreover, provides opportunities for Asian diaspora poets to review and to interact with their cultural traditions in new contexts. In his poem "My Father's Martial Art," Stephen Liu writes,

When he came home Mother said he looked
like a monk and stank of green fungus.
At the fireside he told us about life
at the monastery: his rock pillow,

his cold bath, his steel-bar lifting
and his wood-chopping. He didn't see
a woman for three winters, on Mountain O Mei.

"My Master was both light and heavy.
He skipped over treetops like a squirrel.
Once he stood on a chair, one foot tied
to a rope. We four pulled; we couldn't
move him a bit. His kicks could split
a cedar's trunk."

I saw Father break into a pumpkin
with his fingers. I saw him drop a hawk
with bamboo arrows. He rose before dawn, filled
our backyard with a harsh sound *hah, hah, hah*:
there was his Black Dragon Sweep, his Crane Stand,
his Mantis Walk, his Tiger Leap, his Cobra Coil . . .
infrequently he taught me tricks and made me
fight the best of all the village boys. (1981, 82)

In visual terms, the vivid description of the martial arts can be considered as appealing to the Western gaze, but the representation in Liu's poem, at the same time, seems profoundly to challenge, question, and displace the gaze. In what follows, the focus suddenly blurs, as the "busy street" in an American city is confused with the "high cliffs on O Mei" Mountain in China. Confronting the mainstream "traffic," the "Black Dragon Sweep" as well as the hush "*hah, hah, hah*" seems to be directed toward the gazer:

From a busy street I brood over high cliffs
on O Mei, where my father and his Master sit:
shadows spread across their faces as the smog
between us deepens into a funeral pyre.

But don't retreat into night, my father.
Come down from the cliffs. Come
With a single Black Dragon Sweep and hush
This oncoming traffic with your *hah, hah, hah*. (1981, 83)

What we should note is that the intercultural power relation between the gazer and the gazee has been changed. In Christian Metz's psychoanalytical terms, when the whole system of knowledge is provided by the gazee-analysand, the gazee may also become the gazer-analyser, which can generate a counter-discourse to the intended spectatorship. "As in political struggles," Metz writes, "our only weapons are those of the adversary, as in anthropology, our only source is the native, as in the analytical cure, our only knowledge is that of the analysand, who is also (current French usage tells us so) the analyser [*analysant*]" (1982, 5). In this sense, the speaker's representation of his father's martial arts inscribes a self-reflexive and self-analytical perspective upon his cultural tradition. By brooding over the long shadows of his cultural "master" and "father," the speaker attempts to explore what kind of impact that the old cultural tradition can make upon his life in a modern American society. The efforts "to speak for myself" and "to fight for myself" suggest a kind of critical awareness of the exoticist forces that must be acknowledged before challenged. In this regard, Asian diaspora poems do not simply display a picture of exotic cultures, but rather, they open up a new space in poetic discourse in which different kinds of "gazing" and "gazing-back" are negotiated in relation to cross-cultural contestation.

Asian diaspora poetry raises challenging issues that require us to reimagine the exotic differently and to reconsider the assumptions and meanings of cultural otherness beyond the confines of traditional epistemological hierarchy. "The ongoing process of disruption and manipulation by global discourses," as Rob Wilson and Wimal Dissanayake note, is "rearticulated as a process of translating the transnational structurations of nation, self, and community into 'translational,' *in-between* spaces of negotiated language, borderland being, and bicultural ambivalence" (1996, 2). The cultural identities of Asian diasporas are not fixed or given, but have to be redrawn and renegotiated in relation to each instance of transnational interaction. As a transnational force that traverses different political and economic systems, diaspora challenges existing schemes of interpretation and paradigm of knowledge. As a process in which various dislocated cultural and national presences form new cross-cultural discourses and transform the relationship between the self and the Other, diaspora also disrupts and reconfigures old power relations. "That 'Other' installed in the self thus establishes the permanent incapacity of that 'self' to achieve self-identity," as Judith Butler remarks; "it is as it were always already disrupted by that Other; the disruption of the Other at the heart of the self is the very condition of that self's possibility" (1991, 27). To articulate the Other in diaspora, therefore, means to redefine the "truth" and the "lie" about otherness in new contexts and to re-present the uncanny paradoxical relationship between the self and the Other:

> The other is the truth
> continually denied, a lie only a shade deeper
> than your own. If there were no other
> to pick on, you'd have to invent one. For there is never
> a final solution. (Peeradina 1995, 61)

Chapter Seven

Styling Diasporic Carnival

Performance of Difference

> Carnivalization constantly assisted in the destruction of all barriers . . . ; it brought closer what was distant and united what had been sundered.
>
> Mikhail Bakhtin
>
> *Problems of Dostoevsky's Poetics* (1984, 134–5)

> Within Bakhtin's terminology, style is precisely the form of ideologies.
>
> Ken Hirschkop
>
> "Introduction: Bakhtin and Cultural Theory" (1989, 21)

Mikhail Bakhtin's theory of literary carnival, which has constantly been refined in recent developments of literary and cultural studies, presents a vision of literature as comprising various carnivalizing forces in a process of constant shifts and movements that confront a canonical center. The concept of literary carnivalization, in opposition to canonization and totalization, suggests an interaction among various literary and cultural manifestations. In this sense, Asian diaspora poetry can be considered as embodying a carnivalistic space for performing various cultural differences and literary practices. By associating carnivalistic discourse with diaspora, we will be able to view Asian diaspora poetry in a broad context and to address a few stylistic issues in a new perspective. In a book about postcolonialism, Bill Ashcroft et al. have described a situation that has pointed relevance to our discussion: "This cultural hegemony has been maintained through canonical assumptions about literary activity, and through attitudes to post-colonial literatures which identify them as isolated national off-shoots of English literature, and which therefore relegate them to marginal and subordinate positions"

(1989, 7). The elitist hegemony functions as a canonical filter that operates in literary criticism. The works that happen to pass the filter may receive a kind of recognition, while most of Asian diaspora writings are screened out. As Susan Bassnett has perceived for the study of literatures outside of the canonical center, it is necessary "to start with home culture and to look outwards, rather than to start with the European model of literary excellence and to look inwards" (1993, 38). In our reading of Asian diaspora poetry, we also need to reorient the angle of our perception in order to reconsider the canonizing elitism that still lingers in people's minds. Asian diaspora poetry "has not harvested the amount of critical attention that it truly deserves," as Guiyou Huang notes, "despite the proliferation of a larger number of poets of Asian descent in the twentieth century" (2002, 1). One of the reasons is that Asian diaspora poetry has its unique features and characteristics which cannot fully be explained within the confines of Western poetics. Probably the cultural diversity and stylistic contumacy that we find existing in Asian diaspora poetry can best be examined with reference to Bakhtin's idea of carnival, since it "can be understood only in relation to a set of differences which both oppose it and, at the same time, enable it" (Holquist 1985, 222). For this reason, the concept of carnival provides an important tool for analyzing precisely and deeply the cultural and literary differences within the body of Asian diaspora poetry.

Carnivalistic discourse, according to Bakhtin, suggests a "wild territory" in which the hierarchical domination is toppled down so that the "behavior, gesture and discourse of a person are freed from the authority" of "the all-powerful socio-hierarchical relationships of non-carnival life" (1984, 123). In the absence of a real carnival setting, the wild spirit of carnival has to be expressed in diverse artistic and literary forms. In the process of literary creation, the fragmented, suppressed carnivalistic desire is transformed into viable forms through which a sustained self-validation can be achieved. The obsession with literary innovation and stylistic experimentation, therefore, indicates a transgressive yearning for freedom of traversing various limiting borders. Creation and transgression, as shown in both social and literary sites, challenge and transcend limitation and domination. Artistic innovations and transgression, however, are not purely formal, aesthetic concerns; they are related to other sociocultural practices and issues. The search for appropriate styles to express diasporic experience and anxiety reflects a critical self-consciousness of cultural differences that may be directed to oppose the force of totalizing cultural hegemony. In order to express their cultural differences, Asian diaspora poets break away from the overdetermined discourse of canonical expectation through an act similar to the play of self-staging in a vernacular carnival. In both sociocultural and literary settings, carnival suggests a loosened order and structure, and opens doorways to diverse self-figurations and self-realizations. The experimental poems of Fred Wah, for example, have gone far beyond the conventional boundaries to develop a unique poetic style. Let us quote a few lines from his well-known volume *Breathin' My Name with a Sigh*:

WANT RIVER PIECE OUT OF THIS MOVING RIVER ▇▇▇ TREES BANK
FLOWS ALONGSIDE ▇▇ PASSES BY FLATHEAD THINK ABOUT IT FAR
AWAY IN THE TAMARACK STANDS ▇▇▇▇ NIGHT BURNING
IN THE RIVER ▇ IS A HEAVER, A HEAVEN ▇ ALONG THE ▇▇▇
HORIZON ▇ LANGUAGE COMES ▇▇▇▇▇▇▇▇▇▇ (1981, 40)

Careful readings of Wah's poems reveal that Wah's absorption in poetic experiments, in a sense, reflects his longing for self-expression and self-validation. His artistic play, like carnivals, is a practice of self-staging that expresses symbolically his desire to travel "along the horizon" in search for adequate language to express his diasporic experience. As we know, members of Asian diaspora communities are often divided into different subgroups according to their varying degrees or generations of remove from their countries of origin. In comparison with new immigrants, Wah's relation with his cultural origin is rather remote and the flow of tradition has been interrupted by many kinds of "gaps." However, he faces no less identity problems than others; and as a matter of fact, he has constantly traversed the borders of race, culture, language and history to explore the meanings of his "name" that signifies his cultural roots and identity:

mmmmmm
hm
mmmmmm
hm
yuhh Yeh Yeh
thuh moon
huh^{h} wu wu
unh unh nguh
w_______h
w_______h (1981, 9)

The unique form of this poem expresses his meditation on the "gaps" inscribed in his name. With a feeling of dislocation, Wah tries to establish a self-reflexive dialogue in his poetry that may serve as a bridge to connect the two cultural poles in his life as represented by "w________h." As exemplified by Wah, Asian diaspora poets do not use canonized literary models to authorize their writing, but rather, they take the awareness of their own unusual experiences as a legitimate impetus to poetic innovation. Their enthusiastic engagement with stylistic and formal idiosyncrasy calls for recognition of unconventional interior meanings in their poetic texts that do not accede to the canonized conventions of reading and writing.

In their writings, Asian diaspora poets often express a willful independence from and acute critique of the Western poetic tradition that fails to provide adequate forms for them to express their experiences and feelings. As José Garcia Villa shows in a poem, to follow Western poetic forms rigidly would result only in emptiness, silence and meaninglessness:

> Parenthetical Sonnet
>
> (
>
>) (1988, 85)

The parenthesized space of emptiness, which is supposed to be occupied by fourteen sonnet lines, creates a strong effect of futility. The poet must crack open the parentheses to develop his own form outside of the confines of Western versification—an act of transgression that affirms his speaking subject and constitutes his own assertive difference. Many of Villa's poems represent a strong wish to break away from the fettered convention that suffocates and silences robust self-expressions. Although his form may not look elegant and his cadence may sound stuttering, Villa tirelessly experiments on new manners of expression in his poetry. One of his poems reads:

1

The, circle, is, not, greater,
Than, its, radius,
Which, defines, its, genius.

The, tower, is, not, greater,
Than, its, altitude,
Which, defines, its, solitude.

2

When, Nothing, is, so, well, said,
Or, so, well, done,

It, betrays, itself, and, becomes,
Something:

As, apples, by, Cezanne, or, just,
Lines, by, Mondrian. (1988, 89)

The "stuttering" style seems to suggest a kind of faltering transgression that breaks up the parenthesized space of silence and the resultant excitement with a brand new voice in poetry. The stuttering utterances denaturalize codified language and enact a transgressive performance that refuses to be fettered by given rules and conventions. As Peter Stallybrass observes, "transgression" can be defined "as an operation from the margins, always bordering on silence"; "The carnivalesque becomes identified with the linguistic transgression of the individual artist . . . who confronts the monolithic orthodoxies of the social—that is, individual 'anarchy' subverts collective 'culture'" (1989, 46). In this sense, Villa's poem reflects a carnivalistic rebellion of the dominated against the silence-spell of orthodox norms; and his poem creates an effect of intensive vibration that breaks down the conventional rhythm and measures. His preference of "stuttering" to "sonnetizing" is translated into an effective prosodic strategy that signifies his self-assertion against the domination and totalization of Western poetics.

"The carnivalized text," as Iris Zavala points out, "according to Bakhtin's model, is the meeting ground of a complex semiotic system within a cultural sphere which incorporates linguistic structures and social categories" (1988, 59). To this extent, the concept of carnivalization embodies Bakhtin's most democratic vision of culture and literature as non-hierarchical plural systems. The logosphere of Asian diaspora poetry, in a manner of speaking, provides a carnivalistic space for performing various stylistic and cultural differences. Poetic creation, like carnivalistic performances, is a practice that expresses symbolically the desire for freedom and for diversity. In Mei-Mei Berssenbrugge's works, for example, we find that the complexity of her flowing lines often stretches beyond the limits of conventional poetry to become "formless":

> A flock of birds up acquires the shape of her arcs across the ice, a mirror stage,
> echoing our first misrecognition or the imaginary, to look again and then look,
> so that if he says or she says, my dream about you is older than my knowing you,
> does that mean the dream was dreamed before your meeting him or her?
> The meaning of the dream existed prior to the dream, and then I met you and then I dreamt about you,
> gratifying an enigma that was solved and then posed, with a resulting fullness
> in the dreamer, as with a child to replace himself or replace herself, or as verisimilitude on stage.
> Its story is light that moves from cue to cue as over ground.
> It resembles an arm reaching out to defend you at a sudden stop, but is rhetorical,
> the way your arms full of white down inscribe an immense volume above the ice
>
> (1993, 39)

The "formless" form suggests a spirit of freedom and vividly expresses the poet's vision of "a flock of birds" that constantly change their flight shape as they glide across the ice, playing with our "misrecognition" and challenging us "to look again and then look." Her poem, in a sense, moves away from the structuration of traditional poetry to represent an intense perception of space with long, formless lines. Doing away with the linear mode of conventional lyrics, Berssenbrugge attempts to establish a connection between the external scenery and the inner perception that transcends the formation of our sensory recognition. Berssenbrugge's "invention of long, capacious line," as Linda Voris observes, "has made all the difference in transforming work that might have continued in an expressive, lyrical tradition into an experimental poetics" (2002, 68). Indeed, Berssenbrugge can be regarded as a contemporary maestro of long lines, whose capacious poetry seems to expand the limited space of conventional lyrics to signify a hologramic "fullness" beyond the prosaic "verisimilitude." Like "an arm reaching out," her expansive verse lines creep along the backside of words to diffuse massive significations that cannot be wholly perceived by one steady look. Berssenbrugge's poetic experimentation can be seen clearly with reference to what Zavala describes as "the meeting ground of a complex semiotic system" wherein the linguistic structures, as Lacanian scholars have argued, are related to one's sense of agency and psychic anxiety. Berssenbrugge's poetry can be seen as what Julia Kristeva calls "writing-as-experience-of-limits" (1980b, 137). The exploration of limits suggests a rethinking and interrogating of Western poetic models. Refusing to accept the traditional versification, Berssenbrugge goes on to invent her own language to express her unique sense of agency and psychic anxiety by transgressing the traditional sphere of poetics. Her poetic works such as *Endocrinology* and *Four Year Old Girl* manifest a critique of purist approach to prosody through a carnivalistic combination of linguistic, psychological, scientific, musical, artistic, social and philosophical explorations. As Voris notes, Berssenbrugge's poetry demonstrates, on the one hand, "that the phenomenological world and our imaginative elaboration of it make profound and telling impressions upon us," and on the other hand, "that these experiences, in turn, influence states of self, memory, ideation, and the unconscious in subtle ways that do not depend upon our efforts at containment" (2002, 75).

Like Berssenbrugge, Lawson Fusao Inada also treats poetic creation as a journey of exploration, searching for new forms to express his sense of experience. However, in comparison with Berssenbrugge's philosophizing, Inada's poetry is more action-oriented. Moreover, different from Berssenbrugge's long-lined poetry, some of Inada's pieces appear to be extremely minimal:

Headwaters
Remember
Tradition
Rainbow
Blessing
Daijobu
Headwaters
Incandescent
Incantations
Glistening
Headwaters
Listening

Watching
Feeling
Knowing
Headwaters
Spirits
Rise (1993, 165)

Reading Berssenbrugge's and Inada's poems side by side, readers won't miss the apparent difference. What is not so obvious, however, is the common characteristic that is shared by Berssenbrugge, Inada and other Asian diaspora poets—that is, the persistent experiments on new poetic forms that invite readers to envision the reconnection of language to the world. As Lyn Hejinian says, "Language grants (acknowledges, affirms) and shows (or brings into the space of appearance) what it grants: each utterance is a saying of the phrase 'this is happening'" (2002, 238). What is presented and received through language, however, is already loaded with meanings inherent in the conceptual patterns of a dominant culture. Through dismantling the basic structure of poetry to the bone, Inada endeavors to create new units of meanings, which are close to the oral tradition of Japanese diaspora community. The meaningful weight of Inada's poem stems from his assertion of cultural difference as a performance of language. In this sense, Inada's minimal poem provides an example of poetry-as-action, in which the utterances suggest a fused discourse of speech and action that brings words into being—"listening, watching, feeling, knowing"—"Spirits rise." This is happening and this is action. Inada's poem, which is provocative of the magic power of words, can be regarded as affirmation of a carnivalistic discourse that enchants minimal words with expressive meaningfulness and turns speech into action. Bakhtin describes the discourse of carnivalization as the "transposition of carnival into the language of literature" that brings to literary works the "carnival sense of the world [which] possesses a mighty life-creating and transforming power" (1984, 122 and 107). In this sense, poetry-as-action indicates an active power that gives Asian diaspora poets voice to speak up and, more importantly, in the very act of speaking it constitutes a mode of self-apprehension and self-constituting agency.

To understand Asian diaspora poets' painstaking efforts to develop their own styles and forms, we must be aware of the discursive behavior of cultural hegemony that acts as a ruthless force both to marginalize differences and to constrain individual expressions. In the course of creating an orthodox version of standard language, dominant culture has projected many aspects of irregularity and antigrammaticality on pidgin and other languages used by "outsiders" it deems different and alien. In Asian diaspora poetry, however, the insertion of pidgin or foreign words effectively renders Asian sensibilities into English and signifies different positions of cultural agency. The intermixing of different languages, as a result, adds an extra dimension to Asian diaspora poetry that styles itself as multivalent and polyphonic. In Wing Tek Lum's poems, for example, the use of pidgin and foreign words has created a distinctive style. The poem "T-Bone Steak" reads:

> My father on occasion
> brought home
> one T-bone. *Máang fó, nyùhn*
> *yàuh,* he cautioned:
> heat
> the skillet first,
> the oil you pour just
> before you lay
> the steak on. (1991, 167)

In another piece, "Chinese Hot Pot," Lum writes:

> My dream of America
> is like *dá bìn lòuh*
> with people of all persuasions and tastes
> sitting down around a common pot
> chopsticks and basket scoops here and there
> some cooking squid and others beef
> some tofu or watercress
> all in one broth (1991, 163)

Considered crude and underdeveloped, pidgin nonetheless is more colorful, figurative and expressive than standard English. It is almost unthinkable if diaspora poets never use pidgin in their writings. In some poems, we noted the strategy that mediates and also exposes a striking contrast between the colorful, demotic, culturally rich pidgin and the syntactically advanced yet culturally pale standard English. This incongruity achieves a "picturesque" effect that highlights the cultural landscape of Asian diaspora poetry. As an "aesthetic category celebrating irregularity, discontinuity, variety and unity in composition," opines Lawrence Needham, "the picturesque was a liberal art form that encouraged license within limits, freedom within constraints" (1995, 108). Exploring further along the line of Needham's inquiry, we will reach a new understanding of the picturesque style that constitutes a transgressive, dynamic, carnivalistic discourse—a discourse that gives itself freedom and forcefulness. Lum's poetic language, which intermixes pidgin, dialects and different linguistic registers, is discontinuous and irregular, but it has successfully recaptured Asian diaspora's cultural differences that have been dis(re)membered by the dominant, standard totalizing discourse.

Lum's poetry provides us with valuable insight into the world of language, and helps us discern more clearly the deep connection between the assertion of cultural difference and the performance of language. Lum's determination to reproduce the asyndetic quality of pidgin is not simply a matter of seeking to render non-Western sensibility into English. But rather it should be seen as an expression of carnivalistic desire to resist hierarchical elitism in both poetic and social contexts. Pidgin expressions are often related with the notions of "otherness," which may carry the negative connotation of impurity, heterogeneity and eccentricity. Carnivalistic discourse, however, embraces pidgin language that should not be seen as a passive receptor of social meanings but rather as an active power that allows Asian diaspora poets to achieve self-definition and self-validation. The practice of pidginization, therefore, inscribes a sense of transgression and subversion which, as Bakhtin makes it clear, suggests a suspension of all "hierarchical structure and . . . everything resulting from socio-hierarchical inequality or any other form of inequality among people" (1984, 122–23). From a carnivalistic perspective, we can see, following JanMohamed and Lloyd, "the 'inadequacy' or 'underdevelopment' ascribed to minority texts and authors by a dominant humanism in the end only reveals the limiting (and limited) ideological horizons of that dominant, ethnocentric perspective" (1990, 6). Pidgin language, which is directed against an official language, promises a strong power of carnival in opposition to totalizing ethnocentrism. In this sense, Lum's poetry embodies an awakened consciousness of the power of carnivalistic discourse, which is capable of turning the elements of "inadequacy" and "underdevelopment" into significant cultural difference.

The cultural differences, as represented in Asian diaspora poetry, do not only challenge the homogeneous discourse, but also redefine the tension between the hegemonic culture and the carnivalizing forces that seek to subvert the system of dominating ideology. "In such a relationship," Armstrong and Tennenhouse point out, "even the dominant culture cannot stay the same; it is always negotiating, renegotiating, and absorbing forms of difference" (1989, 21). The renegotiation between the hegemonic culture and various cultural differences lies at the very heart of some poetic works of Asian diaspora writers. It is foregrounded not only as a theme or motif but also inscribed in the very language practice, and it determines how language signifies for different positions of cultural agency. "As the essential medium of subjectivity," says Marina Heung, "language is the ground for playing out cultural differences" (1993, 604). The versification of pidgin and foreign words into poetry gives Asian diaspora poets a sense of identity as well as the power to assert their differences. The picturesque intermixing of languages, therefore, is used as a means to achieve self-definition and self-representation. As Ho Hon Leung writes in "A Symphonic Poem 'Unfinished'":

> I see
> a real 'I' 我
>
> You're a Rose.
> Tho the stem is thorn,
> petals & leaves are strong, colorful
> wine.
>
> Both of us are
> in the West &
> feel bound
> in cells.
>
> The Chinese 'self'—我—
> doesn't have a social image—me—
> as an armour for others
> to judge.
> I me my mine
> 我 我 我 我
> 的 的
>
> If I were Beethoven
> OP. 27
> had to be for you.
>
> The I
> is ready for you
> to read. (1995, 247–248)

By using the Chinese word for "self," Leung foregrounds his deep concern with his ethnic identity and cultural difference as a Chinese diaspora poet.

In Kimiko Hahn's poem "The Izu Dancer," we find that the performance of intermixed languages is related to the assertion of a unique position for the poet to negotiate her gender identity between different cultural traditions:

> Perhaps I didn't want any language. Any marriage.
> Even Kawabata's snowscapes steamed in the winter light.
> Is all betrayal really of father or mother?
> In the kanji for mother
>
> 母
>
> the two nipples reduce it to a primitive symbol.
> I reached to touch with the confidence
> of a child burying into a breast;
> a connection, tangible, but also a perfume
> or stench that is language. Ah,
> the irregular verbs. Oh, yes, the conditional.
> An occasional classical phrase
> nestled into the vernacular.
> The lullabies: should, could, would. I need
> the knowledge from a peach floating down stream:
> *domburikokkosukkou—*
> of saying the right words without thinking. (1992, 91–92)

Both Leung and Hahn question the monolingual model of Western poetics by emphasizing the effects of foreign or "other" linguistic elements in their poetic composition. Their versification, in a sense, can be considered as a cross-cultural performance, in which the interaction among the different cultural presences transrelates various historical, political, and psychological discourses into new forms of identity and fresh expressions of linguistic heteroglossia. The linguistic heteroglossia that we noted in Asian diaspora poetry offers us an innovative and distinctively meaningful poetic mélange, and inscribes a "carnival esthetic" which, to use Ella Shohat's and Robert Stam's words, "rejects formal harmony and unity in favor of the asymmetrical, the heterogeneous, the oxymoronic, the miscegenated" (1994, 302).

In both sociocultural and literary contexts, carnival suggests a loosened order and structure, and opens doorways to self-figuration and self-realization. In order to express their cultural differences, Asian diaspora poets break away from the monologic discourse of dominant language to embrace inter-lingual and cross-cultural interactions. As Marilyn Chin writes in her poem entitled "To Pursue the Limitless,"

> 美言不信 信言不美
>
> *Beautiful words are not truthful*
> *The truth is not beautiful*
>
> You have translated "bitter" as "melon"
> "Fruit" as "willful absence"
>
> You were mum as an egg
> He was brutal as an embryo
> Blood-soup will congeal in the refrigerator
>
> You are both naturalized citizens
> You have the right to a little ecstasy
>
> To (二) err is human
> To (五) woo is woman
>
> *Mái mā*   *Buried mother*
> *Mài má*   *Sold hemp*
> *Mǎi mǎ*   *Bought horse*
>
> No, not the tones but the tomes
> You said My name is *Zhuang Mei*
>   *Sturdy Beauty*
> But he thought you said *Shuang Mei*
>   *Frosty Plum* (2002, 86)

What Chin shows in her poem is an inter-lingual practice that informs and enacts the interstices and overlaps of different cultural and linguistic systems; and more importantly, it suggests different ways of understanding the world, and offers a new poetics that gives voice to the "truth" that "is not beautiful." Linguistic heteroglossia provides us opportunities to pursue for different patterns of understanding and meanings in a "limitless" space beyond the totalizing paradigm of dominant language or monocratic discourse. What we need in today's literary and cultural criticism is a carnivalistic mode of (un)thinking that accommodates rather than reduces the variety of literary and cultural manifestations. This mode of (un)thinking helps us hear the polyphonic voices, perceive heterogeneous performances, and recognize a variety of ways in which cultural and linguistic "systems come to know themselves by playing at being different" (Holquist 1985, 230).

A number of poems by Asian diasporas can be described as picturesque, not only because they contain pidgin English or the intermixing of different languages, but also because they characterize an "irregular" yet dynamic style—a style that grants itself difference and vitality. The following jagged lines are taken from Marilyn Chin's "Rhapsody in Plain Yellow," a poem that obviously deviates from the normal aesthetic etiquette and decorum:

> Say: O celebrator   O celebrant
> of a blessed life, say:
> false   fleeting   hopes
> Say: despair, despair, despair.
> Say: Chinawoman, I am a contradiction in terms:
> I embody frugality and ecstasy.
> Friday Wong dies on a Tuesday,
> O how he loved his lambs.
> He was lost in their sheepfold.
> Say: another mai tai before your death.
> Another   measure another murmur   before your last breath.
> Another boyfriend, Italianesque.
> Say: Save. Exit.
> Say: I am the sentence which shall at last elude her.
> Oh, the hell of heaven's girth, a low mound from here . . .
> Say: Oh, a mother's vision of the emerald hills draws down her brows.
> Say: A brush of jade, a jasper plow furrow.
> Say: ####00000xxxxx!!!!
>
> Contemplate thangs cerebral spiritual open stuff reality
> by definition lack any spatial extension
> we occupy no space and are not measurable
> we do not move undulate are not in perpetual motion
> where for example is thinking in the head? in my vulva?
> (2002, 100–101)

In Chin's poem, the rhapsodic use of language appears to be a powerful style for expressing her carnivalistic sense of the world and identity. By presenting a carnivalistic list of all the contradictions, paradoxes and incongruities in her life, Chin questions the socio-ideological conditions that facilitate the discursive production of identity as well as the meaning production of language. Deferring from the conventional etiquette and decorum of prosody, Chin invents her own rhapsodic style that turns its "irregularity" into a sign of self-assertion, which signifies as well as inscribes her critical consciousness in performing her unique cultural and artistic differences.

Some critics, who may have noticed the rhapsodic use of language, try to draw our attention to the unconventional interior meanings in Asian diaspora poetry that break away from the canonized conventions of reading and writing. As Jeffery Chan et al. observe, "The minority experience does not yield itself to accurate or complete expression in the white man's language. Yet, minority writers, specifically Asian-American writers, are made to feel morally obligated to write in a language produced by an alien and hostile sensibility" (1982, 217). What deserves our further examination, in this regard, is the sociocultural implication of Asian diaspora poets' unprecedented engagement with poetic experimentation and their intention to break through the canonizing power of "elegant" and "correct" English in their attempt to voice their diasporic experience in a transgressive and decanonizing discourse. In Frances Chung's *Crazy Melon and Chinese Apple*, for example, quite a few poems may sound "eccentric." Refusing to subordinate himself to conventional forms of versification, Chung develops his own poetic style that challenges readers' expectation about what a poem should be like. Here is one of his poems:

> *chaúl*
> blue
> Chinese
> Silk (2000, 139)

The power of his eccentric poems subverts prosodic conventions and compels readers to take a new perspective in reading his poetry. Let us read another piece:

> Chinatown Sign
>
> Sweet olives
> 4 for 10¢ (2000, 92)

Chung's odd style confronts what Allon White calls the "'seriousness' of high language." "The social reproduction of seriousness," opines White, "is a fundamental—perhaps *the* fundamental—hegemonic manoeuvre. Once the high language has attained the commanding position of being able to specify what is and is not to be taken *seriously*, its control over the language of its society is virtually assured" (1993, 134). In this context, it is obvious that Asian diaspora poets must develop their own forms of discourse in which their special type of speech can be turned into strategies of self-making representation. Chung's eccentric experimentation registers a carnivalistic language in his writing that affirms his speaking subject and constitutes his own assertive difference. His unserious style, on the one hand, challenges the social and grammatical standards established by the dominant culture, and on the other hand, defies assimilative mimicries and parroting.

If "high" language is one of the means for "hegemonic manoeuvre," the unserious use of language, or slanguage, may indicate Asian diaspora poets' self-conscious resistance against the force of hegemony. "Bakhtin uses 'carnival' to signal all those forms, tropes, and effects in which the symbolic categories of hierarchy and value are inverted" (1993, 7), as Stuart Hall observes. However, carnival "is not simply a metaphor of inversion," Hall hastens to add; "In Bakhtin"s 'carnival,' it is precisely the purity of this binary distinction which is transgressed. The low invades the high, blurring the hierarchical imposition of order; creating, not simply the triumph of one aesthetic over another, but those impure and hybrid forms of the 'grotesque'" (1993, 8). The "impure and hybrid forms of the 'grotesque,'" in the case of Asian diaspora poetry, reflect a critical self-consciousness of difference—linguistic and social—that may be directed to counter the control of totalizing cultural hegemony. John Yau, for example, tries to carnivalize literary language as a gesture of ideological critique of Orientalist cliché. Here is a poem by John Yau:

Moo goo
Milk mush

Guy pan
Piss pot (1996, 105)

This poem is taken from Yau's poetic series "Genghis Chan: Private Eye," which merges the story of the fictitious Charlie Chan with the legend of Mongolian conqueror Genghis Khan. Combining the incongruent images, Yau ridicules the stereotypical representations of "Hollywood Asians." In another piece, Yau writes:

Dimple sample

Rump stump

Dump fun
Dim sum

Slum rubble
Gong sob

Strong song
Oolong

Rinky dink
Trinket rock

Duck walk
Talk muck (1996, 103)

The play of monosyllabic words in the parodic couplets mocks the Hollywood version of Chinese speech in movies. What Yau presents here is an ironic double parody—a parody of Hollywood's parody of Chinese diaspora's pidgin English. The playfulness of Yau's parody suggests a translinguistic practice that has social and political implications, as it jars readers out of complacent habits of thinking and challenges the Orientalist ideology about "Asians" that has long enjoyed a central, totalizing status of popularity in America. Yau refuses to submit himself, on the one hand, to the "tyranny of language" which, to use Jeffery Chan's words, "continues even in the instruments designed to inject the minority into the mainstream" (1982, 217) and, on the other hand, to the stereotypical mode of "Oriental(ist) style." His transgressive use of language is a carnivalistic strategy for performing and legitimating unique cultural difference beyond the stereotyping cliché. His "grotesque" style enables him to break away from the constraints of "high" language and the "official" ideology.

For many Asian diaspora poets, the textual performance has special significance, because the truth of their poems is not merely reported but rather enacted. Put in another way, the formal innovation itself might be performative and allusive, revealing something beneath the textual surface where the signification of a poem does not derive from the verbal denotation, but rather from the imaginative perceptions behind the words within a specific "space of appearance." "That something is occurring," according to Lyn Hejinian, "means it is taking place, or taking a place, in the space of appearance." The "space of appearance" is particularly important in some cases, as "it comes into existence *quâ* context when something is launched in such a way as to become perceptible to us and thereby to involve us" (2002, 237). Some Asian diaspora poems, as it were, are defined and contextualized by their textual appearances. It is significant to note how Asian diaspora poets reshape the Western tradition to launch new varieties of appearance. Let us read, or rather take a look at, Cyn. Zarco's "Magdalena's Vision":

I
loosed
the knot
of cloth
around
his waist
and knelt
at his
feet.
"Father, forgive her for she knows."
I cupped the staff of life and bathed
it lovingly with my cat's tongue. He
rolled his eyes toward Heaven. The
white
cloth
dropped
to the
ground
He filled
my mouth
and drops
of blood
& sweat
fell
from
his
brow.
I
plucked
the crown
of thorns
from
his head

and wiped
his forehead,
the kissed
his face, the
bowl of
his shoulder,
his breasts,
his thighs. . . .

> The skies parted. I freed his feet and hands and sealed his wounds. (1995, 130)

Zarco's practice of textual performance, which draws on the tradition of performative text-making of concrete poetry, poses important questions about some interesting issues. The "appearance" of the poem invites readers to consider the profound implication of Magdalena's vision and refigure it through the perception and experiences of the speaker's, whose voice has ironically been silenced by the hegemony of orthodox culture. "The silent Other of gesture and failed speech," in Bhabha's words, "becomes what Freud calls that 'haphazard member of the herd,' the Stranger, whose languageless presence evokes an archaic anxiety and aggressivity" (1994, 166). Against the monolithic orthodoxy, the poem "loosed the knot of cloth" and made the unusual vision, sensation and knowledge "appear" in front us—so to say, they are "taking place, or taking a place, in the space of appearance." The poet's effort to visualize the "archaic anxiety" through typographical display suggests the necessity to reinvest new meanings in the experience of form. What I find most interesting about the poem, however, is not the vision inside the poem but its textual "appearance," which draws its effect on the cooptive workings of two sign systems. The obvious strength of the poem, in other words, lies in the "languageless presence" with which the speaker evokes the invisible dimensions of her vision, which is accompanied by a paradoxical recognition of the visible. It is through the cooperation of both the verbal and visual performances that the speaker's vision is made accessible to readers and viewers across linguistic barriers. The visual appearance *quâ* context provides a vehicle through which the speaker's knowledge of faith and anxiety are borne across to readers in different cultural and linguistic milieux.

Like Cyn. Zarco, some other Asian diaspora poets also deliberately exploit the possibilities of visual effects in their poetic creation. In her collection *East Wind, West Rain*, Pwu Jean Lee presents an interesting poem entitled "A Guitar":

Her
guitar
has
no
string.
When
she
strums
it,
a thousand silent notes
spring out and calypso in
the corridor of time. Seven
swallows skipping on the
willow tree, the crystal spring
scissored the snowy brook in
the silence of December. As
the pulse of Spring still
slept in the deep veins
of the old oak tree, the
wildwoods budding with ruby
beads trembled in crimson steam.
The white peonies bloomed, withered,
while she sipped Kwan-Yin tea alone.
When the rain-needles pierced into silk
cushion of the painless lake, the railway
stretches her long-empty arms after the
autonomous train. A motherless child,
childless mother sitting on the bench in
the midway of her journey. The Autumn
wind softly asks: Where have you been?
Where is your destination? She takes
a pause at this measure. She is a
silent note at rest in the
song of her life.

(1997, 13)

The peculiar shape of the poem is intended to help us read, view and, most significantly, hear the "silent note" on the speaker's life. In this poem, the seemingly stable boundaries between language, music and painting are dissolved. As the semantic limits of its verbal meaning have been transcended by other modes of expression, the poem seems to perform a sonatina of diasporic life—"Where have you been? Where is your destination?" Crossing both spatial and temporal borders, the poem pushes the limits of textuality into a "corridor of time" where "a thousand silent notes spring out"—a soundless symphony of polyphonic voices and heterogeneous performances. It seems to be a musical carnival in imagination and a calypso in fantasy. Lee's determination to make a song out of silent notes and to turn silence into meaningful expressions can be regarded as an affirmation of carnivalistic discourse that opens up a space of resonance and reverberation. Refusing to play monotonous and monological tunes, Asian diaspora poets are enthusiastic in exploring new possibilities in their poetry and constantly producing fresh pieces that we never heard before.

Asian diaspora poets work with two different spheres of culture between Asia and America and, as a result, they must restructure epistemologically two sets of perception. The two spheres depend on each other for meaning production by locking them into a mutually-defining relationship, which is not based on mutually exclusive oppositions but on interactions. In Bakhtin's terms, the process of cross-cultural interaction can be described as dialogic in that it suggests a way of localizing the ground of meaning production at the intersection of different patterns of understanding. As Roy Miki presents in his poem,

> localism in linguistic ineptitude
> such rude awakening to surge
> control produces perception
>
>   eg
>   the camellia strewn
> on the ground
>
>   in disarray with
>   its nectar sucked out
>
> is a blind corner turned too
> late in the smoke screen—
>
> the attitude of
> more can do
>
>   (can do?)

— — — —
— — — —
sea — — — —
— — — — —
— — — shore —
— — — —
— crossing — —
— — — — — (1995, 284)

Writing from two shores and mediating across two spheres, Miki expresses his anxiety about "linguistic ineptitude" that characterizes an ambiguous dimension of Asian diaspora poetry. In a sense, dialogic interaction means to work from a position within both spheres and yet not totally within either, pointing to their own inherent "blind corners" and "smoke screens." Moving back and forth between different sets of perception, Asian diaspora poets may encounter various gaps, crossings and links. "At points of linkage," as Lyn Hejinian points out, "the possibility of a figure of contradiction arises: a figure we might call by a Greek name, *xenos*. *Xenos* means 'stranger' or 'foreigner,' but more importantly, from *xenos* two English words with what seem like opposite meanings are derived: they are guest and host" (2002, 235). In the case of Asian diaspora poets, the paradox is that they have an ambiguous identity as both guest and host—the paradoxical position enables Asian diaspora poets to work within and yet not totally within a discourse that they both develop and subvert. Probably the ambiguity is best expressed in Myung Mi Kim's work, which vividly records her experience and thinking as a "perpetual foreigner." Kim regards herself as a foreigner not in the sense that she is a diaspora poet of Korean descent, but rather for the reason that she refuses to translate herself into a discourse in which she does not feel at home. In other words, Kim tries to express her experience and perception beyond the common sense of familiar language and, as a result, her poetic work does not yield to easy interpretation in Western poetics. In "Anna O Addendum," Kim writes:

Pole stricken mulishly copy
                    Scribe   ion   order
When fury
To full sum
          Summon deluge
Come now and hear
                    Picture more at variance

•

Augment morning arriving ensnare
Records civil
            Recourse stir sterile jar fir
Can't see the rain or the plow
                                    Unwarranted tended
Privation gnarled
            Lost conversations (1995, 361–362)

Echoing Miki's concern with "linguistic ineptitude," Kim's poem foregrounds the issue of "unintelligibility" in a broad sociocultural context, and explores how the question of language reveals multifaceted relationships of power, ideology and representation. In the very beginning of her poem, Kim includes a passage from Freud's case study of "Fraulein Anna O" as epigraph: "In the process of time she became almost entirely deprived of words. She put them together laboriously out of four or five languages and became almost unintelligible" (1995, 360). What Kim represents in her poetry, which is characterized by discontinuous speeches and fragmented images, is often the raw materials or rather materiality of language with densely layered referentialities to political, social and historical forces, which render less powerful peoples, languages and cultures unintelligible and inarticulate. Kim's poetry implicates a tendency to expose the concealed frames of intelligibility and to express new forms of cultural enunciation against the conventional scheme of interpretation. Kim's concern with the unintelligible, the muted and the inarticulate may remind us of what José Garcia Villa said before: "Poetry is a struggle between a word and silence" (1962, 224). Although the situation has been changing, for poets of Asian diaspora communities, the task of struggling against silence seems no less urgent and pressing.

"The language of poetry is a language of inquiry," as Hejinian remarks; "To experience is to go through or over the limit (the word comes from the Greek *peras*—term, limit)" (2002, 240). The idiosyncratic performances and experiments have special significance for Asian diaspora poetry, since they provide a discursive space where the disembodied cultural differences can be reconstructed into new forms. "The aim of cultural difference," as Bhabha opines, "is to rearticulate the sum of knowledge from the perspective of the signifying position of the minority that resists totalization" (1994, 162). The development of a unique cultural consciousness is fundamental to a minority or "subaltern" group of poets whose textual performances, in Gayatri Spivak's words, can be described "in terms of reversing, displacing and seizing the apparatus of value-coding" (1990, 228). The "subaltern" that is silenced by the hegemony of language and culture must speak up in its own voice. Spivak's idea suggests a carnivalistic discourse of heteroglossia that articulates and affirms cultural and artistic diversity. In this sense, Asian diaspora poetry inscribes a rebellion inside their textual dynamics against the "hegemonic manoeuvre" of "high" language and culture that marginalizes and ostracizes "alien," "eccentric" discourses. In Julia Kristeva's words, "carnivalesque discourse breaks through the laws of a language censored by grammar and semantics and, at the same time, is a social and political protest" (1980, 65). Asian diaspora poets attempt to carnivalize prosodic conventions in order to stage their diasporic experiences that have never been expressed in canonic cliché. For this reason, they cannot follow the "grammar" of Western poetics that produces homogenizing and stifling effects on "alien," "eccentric" cultural sensibilities. As Rita Wong describes in her "grammar poem":

> write around the absence, she said, show
> its existence
> demonstrate *this is*
> its contours *the sound of*
> how it *my chinese tongue*
> tastes *whispering:* nei tou
> where gnaw ma? *no*
> its edges *tones can*
> fall *urvive this*
> hard *alphabet*
> on my stuttering tongue, how its tones &
> pictograms get flattened out by the
> steamroller of the english language,
> *live* its etymology of
> *half-submerged* assimilation
> *in the salty home of* tramples budding
> *my mother tongue,* memory into sawdusty
> *shallows* stereotypes, regimented capitals,
> arrogant nouns & more nouns,
> punctuated by subservient descriptors.
> grammar is the dust on the streets waiting to be washed off
> by immigrant cleaners or blown into your eyes by the wind. grammar
> is the invisible net in the air, holding your words in place. grammar,
> like wealth, belongs in the hands of the people who produce it. (1999, 23)

Wong's poem seems to challenge the social and "grammatical" standards established by the dominant culture. Since "grammar, like wealth, belongs in the hands of the people who produce it," the speaker would rather see "grammar" as "the dust on the streets waiting to be washed off by immigrant cleaners." Since "high" language is one of the major expressions of "hegemonic manoeuvre," the ideological positions of Asian diaspora poets are also reflected in their use of "unserious" and "ungrammatical" language. The discord between the "seriousness" of official language and the "playfulness" of poetic ungrammaticality suggests a translinguistic practice that has social and political implications. "Rhetoric and the regularities of language and discourse were no less than the structure of the dominant social order," as Peter Stallybrass remarks; "linguistic transgression became a privileged form of politics, since it violated the very terrain on which more conventional political activity was always already situated" (1989, 45). The "ungrammatic" style that Wong chooses for her poetry breaks away from the constraints of "high" language and the "official" discourse. In an unfettered textual practice, Asian diaspora poetry encompasses various kinds of dynamic "irregularity" and "ungrammaticality" as an assertion of carnivalistic freedom. Asian diaspora poetry demonstrates how artistic performances are capable of creative self-preservation and reinvention, offering new ways to style individual and cultural differences.

"Within Bakhtin's terminology," as Ken Hirschkop points out, "style is precisely the form of ideologies, which tells us something quite important about them: that they exist in social, semiotic form, and that they are dialogical in nature, defined by their necessary relation to opposing and alternative ideologies" (1989, 21). In the process of styling itself, Asian diaspora poetry claims a new space for heteroglossical utterances and subverts the dominant "apparatus of value-coding." Competing against the canonizing power of "elegant," "high" English, the carnivalistic discourse of heteroglossia articulates and affirms diverse cultural values and literary representations. Carnivalistic discourse, according to Kristeva, is "transgression giving itself a law" (1980a, 71). The concept of literary carnivalization, in opposition to canonization and totalization, suggests an interaction among various literary manifestations without the polarity of high/low or central/marginal: "The low is thus no longer the mirror-image subject of the high, waiting in the wings to substitute it . . . but another related but different figure" (Hall 1993, 9). The carnivalistic discourse, moving beyond the simplistic binary structure, informs and enacts the interstices and overlaps of different literary practices and their shared differences. In his collection of poetry, *Outspeaks: A Rhapsody*, Albert Saijo attempts to develop a carnivalistic style of rhapsody, a truly democratic grammar of slanguage in which there is "NO FORMAL-VERNACULAR OR DEMOTIC-HIERATIC OPPOSITION" (1997, 73).

The carnivalistic rhapsody, in a sense, can be regarded as a poetic affirmation of difference against the domination and totalization of monolithic orthodox culture; and for this reason, carnivalistic discourse implicates an active power that allows Asian diaspora poets to achieve self-definition and self-validation. Asian diaspora poetry, however, does not entirely negate the Western poetic tradition, but rather plays with it parodically. Starting from a marginal position, Asian diaspora poetry has been undergoing a long process in which it slowly legitimates the existence of its own styles against "the limiting (and limited) ideological horizons." Moreover, as the notion of carnival suggests, Asian diaspora poetry itself is not pure or monolithic, but rather multivalent and polyphonic. As both Asia and America are rapidly fragmented and diluted in the age of globalization, Asian diaspora poetry has continued to develop itself, absorbing new forms of difference and fashioning new practices of creation. Today, Asian diaspora poetry as a whole can best be conceived carnivalistically. It *is* a carnival.

Chapter Eight

Conclusion

Journey without Maps

> Caught between mimicry, alterity and ultimately silence, I write from two shores and between two cultures.
>
> Iain Chambers
>
> *Border Dialogues* (1990, 13)

> The story never stops beginning or ending. It appears headless and bottomless for it is built on differences.
>
> Trinh T. Minh-ha
>
> *Woman, Native, Other* (1989, 2)

Regarding his journey as a diaspora poet, Arthur Sze tells us that his "poetry is exemplified by the character of *xuan*" in Chinese, which is derived from dyeing. "The character itself depicts silk dipped below ground level into an indigo vat; the silk hangs from a pole into the dye bath." What Sze tries to show is the process of transformation implicated in the idea of *xuan*: "When the silk is pulled up into the air, it is at first a greenish color. The yarn begins to turn blue because chemicals in the dye oxidize when they come in contact with oxygen in the air" (1999, 74). The multilayered colors of *xuan*, as it were, inspire Sze to create "poems that are not one-dimensional; they are multidimensional and challenge the reader to stretch and grow" (1999, 74). Let us quote a few lines from his poem "The Silk Road":

> The, a, this, the, tangerine, splash, hardly:
> these threads of sound may be spun in s-spin into fiber:
>
> lighted buoy, whistling buoy, spar buoy, bell buoy, buoy.

Hear the sounds of apricots dropping from branches to the earth;

feel the red vibration of wings before you see a hummingbird.
A man may travel from Mindanao to Macau to avoid

staring into himself; he may search at night in a helicopter
for the shimmer of a fire opal dropped into water;

he may inhale starlight as if it were a pungent yellow
flower opening slowly in the still August night. (1995, 14)

Sze invites readers to journey with him—not exactly along the historical "silk road" but rather along the variable paths of his imagination to establish new connections among the multiple layers of human existence. In addition, the journey includes numerous detours through other places, real or imagined. To a certain extent, Sze's poetry represents a nonlinear/multilinear or non-sequential/multisequential web in which the nuclear tests on Bikini Island can be connected with the "apricots dropping from branches" in China. "My poems," as Sze tells us, "ask a reader to read and reread, to experience the layering of our existence, and to embark on a transformational process. I believe there are many readers willing to make this journey" (1999, 74). It is a transformational journey that asserts multiple connections among different cultures. The multidimensional space and temporality inscribed in Sze's poetry disrupt the apparent closure of nationality and allude to transnational communities where the local and the global encounter as contiguous neighbors. "Like it or not," in Sze's opinion, "we live in a complex world. (I take the word *complex* to be derived from *plex*, "to braid," and *com*, meaning 'with' or 'together.') We live a world in which the interactions of different cultures have the possibility of each enriching the other; let us not deny ourselves this opportunity" (1999, 76). As Sze shows in his poem "Archipelago," what would seem to be unconnected events, activities and images in remote areas might be linked or linkable within a web of global signification. The speaker's visit to a Ryoanji temple in Kyoto, for instance, is somehow connected across geographical and temporal distance with a ceremony that takes place in a pueblo in New Mexico:

I walk along the length of a stone-and-gravel garden
and feel without looking how the fifteen stones
appear and disappear. I had not expected the space
to be defined by a wall made of clay boiled in oil

> nor to see above a series of green cryptomeria
> pungent in spring. I stop and feel an April snow
> begin to fall on the stones and raked gravel and see
> how distance turns into abstraction desire and ordinary
> things: from the air, corn and soybean fields are
> a series of horizontal and vertical stripes of pure color:
> viridian, yellow ocher, raw sienna, sap green. I
> remember in Istanbul at the entrance to the Blue Mosque
> two parallel, extended lines of shoes humming at
> the threshold of paradise. Up close, it's hard to know
> if the rattle of milk bottles will become a topaz,
> or a moment of throttled anger tripe that is
> chewed and chewed. In the distance, I feel drumming
> and chanting and see a line of Pueblo women dancing
> with black-on-black jars on their heads; they lift
> the jars high then start to throw them to the ground. (1995, 75)

The juxtaposition of disparate occurrences and incidents communicates Sze's view of the world as a complex web of interconnected multiplicity. To this extent, Sze's poetry reflects the global consciousness of a diaspora poet, for whom the "ongoing dialogue" across the borders and limits of cultures, languages and nations "is essential for insight." In his poetry, Sze journeys beyond the patrimonial boundaries of singular cultures. "To say a multicultural writer/artist is totally and exclusively answerable to his or her ethnic community, must be the spokesperson of that community," in Sze's opinion, "can lead to terribly reductive consequences" (1999, 75).

For Sze, diaspora is associated with the sense of displacement and uprootedness, but it also implicates a process of crossing various kinds of limitations and suggests a vastness of new creativity beyond national borders. As Sze's poetry suggests, although the notion of national literature is by no means out of date, there are new pressures and demand being put on the reconceptualization of inter-national literature that has developed significantly in the process of worldwide diaspora. Asian diaspora poetry, in this regard, presents challenging questions in the era of globalization, and urges us to explore and to theorize the discourse of inter-national literature whose cultural dimensions have gone far beyond the borders of nation-states. Whether in theoretical or practical terms, we should not ignore the fact that the production, reception and consumption of Asian diaspora poetry in a cross-cultural and transnational context have unlocked new forms and expressions of global and local negotiation. As a result of the interaction between different systems of cultures, Asian diaspora poetry has disrupted the existing paradigms of signification, triggering them to take on new configurations. In "a world where cross-cultural contact can no longer be ignored," as Claire Sponsler points out, we have to recognize "both the persistence and the importance of this flow of cultures, peoples, and ideas across the borders that themselves are product of conceptual and ideological as much as geographic strategies of containment" (2000, 1). Asian diaspora poetry, to a certain degree, epitomizes the interaction among differential global and local discourses that transrelates various cultural, historical, political and psychological presences into deterritorialized constructions, which demand and activate decentered transnational communication and community. Furthermore, it suggests a new way of thinking.

"Our academic discourse of 'diaspora,'" says Stephen Sumida, "recognizes those global migrants nowadays who can sustain a sense that they are participating in 'two cultures' simultaneously, 'in real time'" (2000, 109). What I find most interesting about the idea of simultaneous participation is that the different versions of "real time" exerted in discrete pscychio-cultural locales actually implicate a temporal disjuncture between different cultural frames, which causes Asian diaspora poets to assume an ambiguous position in their attempt to link their cultural inheritances with the new developments of globalization. "In the double movement of globalisation," says Iain Chambers, "there can emerge counter-histories," "counter-memories," "and counter-communities" "that persist in the counter-discourse of a nonlinear or syncopated understanding of modernity" (1996, 53). The "syncopated understanding" is of essential importance for Asian diaspora poetry, since the global flows of diaspora have compressed various local tempos into a global space of cross-cultural encounter and negotiation. According to Mike Featherstone, it is the "effects of time-space compression" that make possible the "simultaneous transactions which sustain deterritorialized cultures" (1996, 61). In this regard, what Asian diaspora poetry shows is the powerful "effects" of deterritorialized cultures, which rest upon a sustained transnational force directed to our deeply felt experiences of simultaneity in the era of globalization. The experiences of simultaneity have also brought out a vision of permeable relationship between cultures and nations. In a sense, diaspora can be considered as an impetus to the process of "denationalization" which, as Sau-ling Wong points out, "entails a relaxation of the distinction between what is Asian American and what is 'Asian'" (1995, 5). Wong's observation about the "increased porosity between Asian and Asian American" draws our attention to the fact that as mutual penetration has become an increasingly important characteristic of our era, it is increasingly difficult to draw the division between Asia and America and between the global and the local. At such a historic moment, Asian diaspora poetry reflects the growing complexity of the interaction as well as the permeability between different national and cultural forces, highlighting the conditions that have expanded the "in-between space that provides the most common terrain on which the debates over globalization have taken place, usually framed as a relation between the national and the international, projected toward a new transnational context" (Grossberg 1996, 172). Since diaspora means both border-crossing and border-redefining in spatial and temporal domains, the so-called "scattered historical inheritance" and "heterogeneous present" are often transrelated and translocated in a paradoxical communication of "global latency" and "local particularity." To write in diaspora requires one to rearticulate local particularity in both transnational and transcultural terms. As John Hawley observes, on the one hand, the "sense of interconnection between cultures, in which an increasing percentage of the globe has immediate and overlapping access to artifacts produced by disparate and often conflictive systems of meaning"; and on the other hand, the "sense of manifest particularity" that "resists such deconstruction, implying stasis and essential difference as possibilities" (1996, 1). The two senses, which are inscribed in a process of diaspora across cultural and national borders, indicate an ambivalent characteristic of cultural rearticulations in Asian diaspora poetry.

Cultural rearticulations implicate change, transformation and appropriation of a culture in different sociopolitical contexts. As a consequence of the negotiation of different systems of social signification, cultural rearticulation may take on special significance in a transnational space. The struggle for a new system of cultural rearticulation has forced the old divide between the global and the local to break down. Nonetheless, this does not mean that the demarcation line between the two sides disappears, but that a new interstitial and overlapping border must be re-established, and a new balance between "global latency" and "local particularity" must be revalidated. In a broad perspective, Asian diaspora poetry can be seen as embodying a paradoxical combination of two forces. On the one hand, globalism disrupts the apparent closure of nationality and generates transnational communications and communities; and on the other hand, localism invokes the discourse of political and cultural particularity. In terms of poetic creation, the two processes—the globalization of the local and the localization of the global—are not antithetical but rather convoluted in ever changing configurations. Henri Lefebvre's theory of "differential space" might be helpful for us to imagine how the global and the local interact within a correlative contraposition. What Lefebvre tries to assert is a paradox: on the one hand, we need to envisage a mutually supplementary correlation between the "global (or conceived) space" and the "fragmented (or directly experienced) space" (1991, 355); and on the other, we should not ignore the tension and its resultant complexity that exist within either of the spaces. What has emerged from this situation is a new global-conscious localism in literature, which correlates with the current international racing for cultural rearticulation. This global-conscious localism interacts and engages with the global discourse, operating within the very system it attempts to subvert. It suggests a self-reflexive strategy by which Asian diaspora poets are able to resignify the assumptions and meanings of deterritorialized Asian cultures. In her poem "Summer Sonatina," Marilyn Chin writes:

> Some American poet said to me, *The Haiku is dead.*
> I thought, *pink and swollen, something sad about his body.*
>
> He said, *The Tao is untranslatable and the Haiku is dead.*
> I thought, *pink and swollen, something sad about his body.*
>
> ———
>
> *The poet guards the conscience of society*—no, you're wrong,
> She stands lonely on that hillock observing the pastures.
> The world scoffs back with bog and terror.
> Fake paradise, imported palmettos,
> O Prince, do not lose your soul in the ramparts.
> West of Chin's edge, there are no new friends. (2002, 90–91)

The inter-view between the American poet and the speaker enacts a paradoxical play of interreference between American and Asian literary inheritances, which reveals the speaker's awareness of "fake paradise" and "imported palmettos" that exist in current cultural articulation. The two sides, moreover, do not produce a symmetric binary operation, but rather enact a cross-cultural negotiation. The condescending lament on the death of *Haiku* is indicative of the pressure of global totality that has been represented by the spreading of Western norms as "common sense." Writing against the common sense, Chin's persona asserts her cultural distinctiveness and imagines herself as a "lonely" figure—"She stands lonely on that hillock observing the pastures"—who seems to be situated on the unsettling "edges" of different cultural spheres.

Caught between disparate sociocultural spheres that cannot be fully integrated into each other, Asian diaspora poetry is subject to a process of constant resignification between different cultural traditions. In Shirley Lim's "An Immigrant Looks at Whitman," we read:

> Something wonderful and different
> Might turn to memorialize
> The wide water of his death.
> Second death. There are earthquakes
> Daily. Bombs go off and little-
> Known shop-girls are blown away,
> Chin off, legs off at the knee.
>
> The major prophets gazing upwards
> Saw celestial maze, dark redoubts,
> Not the saw-whet owl or long
> Purples deep in marshes.
> But, for you, bring golden pheasant,
> Goldenrod, my Asia, my America.
> I fish in the Great Lakes inwards,
> Forsaking gods for leeches and wild pansy. (1994, 91)

Lim's poem suggests an ambivalent space of splitting and overlapping that marks the diasporic identification with an inter-national linkage between Whitman and the immigrant speaker. "Forsaking gods" as the point of reference, the speaker is determined to search for her own sense of "America" and sensibility of "Asia" in a wide "maze" beyond territorial and temporal limitations. "Being Asian," as Ien Ang remarks, "means being non-Western, at least from the dominant point of view, and this in itself has strong implications for one's sense of self, especially if one is (positioned as) Asian in the West" (2001, 4). Relating Ang's observation to Lim's poem, we may note that what the speaker claims to be her "Asia" actually refers to the deterritorialized Asian sensibility which, nonetheless, cannot be melted into the generosity of American sense. Lim's poem, therefore, is not merely a representation of immigrant experience in America, but rather an investigation into the negotiation between different cultural values and traditions beyond the boundaries of narrowly defined "Asia" and "America." The conceptual entities of "Asia" and "America," moreover, are not posited as dualistic, oppositional and completely separate, but rather, they are in a process of constant dilution, fragmentation and transformation. To be in diaspora means to challenge the delimited. Today, as cultural interchange and exchange advance rapidly, the study of Asian diaspora poetry demands vigorous examination of the changing mechanism of the international flows of various deterritorialized cultures. Breaking the "barriers of thought and experience" and mediating between the "scattered cultural inheritance" and the "heterogeneous present," Asian diaspora poetry does not indicate a site of belonging but rather a process of becoming. Traveling with these wonderful poets, we will move out of the blind corners of our racial and cultural ghettos towards a new land of diasporic poetics, whose topography and dimensions have not yet been fully recognized or mapped in critical terms.

Bibliography

Ahmed, Sara. 1999. "Home and Away: Narratives of Migration and Estrangement." *International Journal of Cultural Studies* 2: 329–347.

Alexander, Meena. 1999. "Indian April." In *The NuyorAsian Anthology: Asian American Writings about New York City*, ed. Bina A. Realuyo. New York: Asian American Writers' Workshop. 262–265.

———.1998. "Golden Horizon." In *Black Lightning: Poetry-in-progress*, ed. Eileen Tabios. New York: Asian American Writers' Workshop. 207–208.

Ang, Ien. 2001. *On Not Speaking Chinese: Living between Asia and the West*. London and New York: Routledge.

Anzaldúa, Gloria. 1987. *Borderlands/La Frontera: The New Mestiza*. San Francisco: Aunt Lute Books.

Armstrong, Nancy, and Leonard Tennenhouse, eds. 1989. *The Violence of Representation: Literature and the History of Violence*. London and New York: Routledge.

Ashcroft, Bill, Gareth Griffiths and Helen Tiffin, eds. 1989. *The Empire Writes Back: Theory and Practice in Post-colonial Literatures*. London and New York: Routledge.

Bacalzo, Dan. 2000. "I'm Sorry, But I don't Speak the Language." In *Take Out: Queer Writing from Asian Pacific America*, ed. Quang Bao and Hanya Yanagihara. New York: Asian American Writers' Workshop. 33–34.

Bakhtin, Mikhail. 1984. *Problems of Dostoevsky's Poetics*, ed. and trans. Caryl Emerson. Minneapolis: University of Minnesota Press.

———.1981. *The Dialogic Imagination: Four Essays*, ed. Michael Holquist, and trans. Caryl Emerson and Michael Holquist. Austin: University of Texas Press.

Bachelard, Gaston. 1969. *The Poetics of Space*, trans. Maria Jolas. Boston: Beacon Press.

Bannerji, Himani. 1990. "To Sylvia Plath." In *Shakti's Words: An Anthology of South Asian Canadian Women's Poetry*, eds. Diane McGifford and Judith Kearns. Toronto: TSAR. 12.

———.1990. "Wife." In *Shakti's Words: An Anthology of South Asian Canadian Women's Poetry*, eds. Diane McGifford and Judith Kearns. Toronto: TSAR. 3.

Basch, Linda, Nina Glick Schiller, and Cristina Szanton Blanc, eds. 1994. *Nation Unbound: Transnational Projects, Postcolonial Predicaments and Deterritorialized Nation-States*. Langhorne, PA: Gordon and Breach.

Bassnett, Susan. 1993. *Comparative Literature: A Critical Introduction*. Oxford, UK and Cambridge, MA: Blackwell.

Berssenbrugge, Mei-Mei. 1998. "Kali." In *Four Year Old Girl*. Berkeley, CA: Kelsey St. Press. 71–77.

———.1993. "The Swan." In *The Open Boat: Poems from Asian America*, ed. Garrett Hongo. New York: Anchor. 38–39.

Bertman, Stephen. 2000. *Cultural Amnesia: America's Future and the Crisis of Memory*. Westport, CT and London: Praeger.

Bhabha, Homi. 1995. "Freedom's Basis in the Indeterminate." In *The Identity in Question*, ed. John Rajchman. London and New York: Routledge. 47–62.

———. 1994. *The Location of Culture*. London and New York: Routledge.

———.1990. "DissemiNation: Time, Narrative, and the Margins of the Modern Nation." In *Nation and Narration*, ed. Homi Bhabha. London and New York: Routledge. 291–322.

Bottomley, Gillian. 1992. *From Another Place: Migration and the Politics of Culture*. Cambridge: Cambridge University Press.

Butler, Judith. 1991. "Imitation and Gender Subordination." In *Inside/Out: Lesbian Theories, Gay Theories*, ed. Diana Fuss. London and New York: Routledge. 13–31.

Casey, Edward S. 1997. *The Fate of Place*. Berkeley: University of California Press.

———. 1987. *Remembering: A Phenomenological Study*. Bloomington: Indiana University Press.

Chambers, Iain. 1996. "Signs of Silence, Lines of Listening" In *The Post-Colonial Question: Common Skies, Divided Horizons*, eds. Iain Chambers and Lidia Curti. London and New York: Routledge. 47–64.

———.1994. *Migrancy, Culture, Identity*. London and New York: Routledge.

———.1990. *Border Dialogues: Journey in Postmodernity*. London and New York: Routledge.

Chan, Jeffery Paul, et al. 1982. "An Introduction to Chinese-American and Japanese-American Literatures." In *Three American Literatures*, ed. Houston A. Baker, Jr. New York: MLA. 197–228.

Chang, Diana. 1983. "Second Nature." In *Breaking Silence: An Anthology of Contemporary Asian American Poets*, ed. Joseph Bruchac. Greenfield Center, NY: The Greenfield Review Press. 20.

———.1974. "Otherness." In *Asian-American Heritage: An Anthology of Prose and Poetry*, ed. David Hsin-fu Wand. New York: Washington Square Press. 135–136.

Chang, Gordon H., ed. 2001. *Asian Americans and Politics: An Exploration.* Stanford: Stanford University Press.

Chang, Robert. 1997. "A Meditation on Borders." In *Immigrants Out! The New Nativism and the Anti-immigrant Impulse in the United States*, ed. Juan F. Perea. New York and London: New York University Press. 244–253.

Cheng, Sait Chia. 1981. *Turned Clay*. Halifax: Fiddlehead.

Cheung, King-kok. 1997. "Re-viewing Asian American Literary Studies." In *An Interethnic Companion to Asian American Literature*, ed. King-kok Cheung. Cambridge: Cambridge University Press. 1–38.

Chiang, Fay. 1999. "For Those Who Run Away from the Movement." In *The NuyorAsian Anthology: Asian American Writings about New York City*, ed. Bino A. Realuyo. New York: Asian American Writers' Workshop. 326–329.

Chin, Marilyn. 2002. "The Colonial Language Is English." In *Rhapsody in Plain Yellow*. New York and London: W. W. Norton. 20–21.

———.2002. "To Pursue the Limitless." In *Rhapsody in Plain Yellow*. New York and London: W. W. Norton. 85–87.

———.2002. "Summer Sonatina." In *Rhapsody in Plain Yellow*. New York and London: W. W. Norton. 90–91.

———.2002. "Rhapsody in Plain Yellow." In *Rhapsody in Plain Yellow*. New York and London: W. W. Norton. 96–103.

———.1994. "How I Got that Name." In *The Phoenix Gone, The Terrace Empty*. Minneapolis: Milkweed Editions. 16–18.

———.1994. "Composed Near the Bay Bridge." In *The Phoenix Gone, The Terrace Empty*. Minneapolis: Milkweed Editions. 80.

Chow, Rey. 2002. *The Protestant Ethnic and the Spirit of Capitalism*. New York: Columbia University Press.

———.1998. *Ethics after Idealism: Theory-Culture-Ethnicity-Reading*. Bloomington: Indiana University Press.

———.1995. *Primitive Passions: Visuality, Sexuality, Ethnography, and Contemporary Chinese Cinema*. New York: Columbia University Press.

———.1993. *Writing Diaspora: Tactics of Intervention in Contemporary Cultural Studies*. Bloomington: Indiana University Press.

Chuh, Kandice. 2003. *Imagine Otherwise: On Asian Americanist Critique*. Durham and London: Duke University Press.

Chung, Frances. 2000. "chaúl." In *Crazy Melon and Chinese Apple*, compiled and with an Afterword by Walter K. Lew. Middletown, CT: Wesleyan University Press. 139.

———.2000. "Chinatown Sign." In *Crazy Melon and Chinese Apple*, compiled and with an Afterword by Walter K. Lew. Middletown, CT: Wesleyan University Press. 92.

Clifford, James. 1997. *Routes: Travel and Translation in the Late Twentieth Century*. Cambridge, MA: Harvard University Press.

———.1988. *The Predicament of Culture: Twentieth-Century Ethnography, Literature and Art.* Cambridge, MA: Harvard University Press.

Cohen, Robin. 1997. *Global Diaspora: An Introduction.* Seattle: University of Washington Press.

Crusz, Rienzi. 1996. "The Rain doesn't Know Me Any More." In *Another Way to Dance: Contemporary Asian Poetry from Canada and the United States*, ed. Cyril Dabydeen. Toronto: TSAR. 48–49.

———.1996. "Where Adam First Touched God." In *Another Way to Dance: Contemporary Asian Poetry from Canada and the United States*, ed. Cyril Dabydeen. Toronto: TSAR. 45–46.

Davey, Frank. 1993. *Post-National Arguments: The Politics of the Anglophone Canadian Novel Since 1967.* Toronto: University of Toronto Press.

Deleuze, Gilles, and Félix Guattari. 1987. *A Thousand Plateaus: Capitalism and Schizophrenia*, trans. Brian Massumi. Minneapolis: University of Minnesota Press.

Derrida, Jacques. 1998. *Monolingualism of the Other, or, The Prosthesis of Origin*, trans. Patrick Mensah. Stanford: Stanford University Press.

———.1979. "Living On: Border Lines," trans. James Hulbert. In *Deconstruction and Criticism*, eds. Harold Bloom, et al. London: Routledge and Kegan Paul. 75–176.

Engkent, Garry. 1991. "Why My Mother Can't Speak English." In *Many-Mouthed Birds: Contemporary Writing by Chinese Canadians*, eds. Bennett Lee and Jim Wong-Chu. Vancouver and Toronto: Douglas and McIntyre. 9–16.

Espinet, Ramabai. 1991. "In the Jungle." In *Many-Mouthed Birds: Contemporary Writing by Chinese Canadians*, eds. Bennett Lee and Jim Wong-Chu. Vancouver and Toronto: Douglas and McIntyre. 38–39.

Featherstone, Mike. 1996. "Localism, Globalism, and Cultural Identity." In *Global/Local: Cultural Production and the Transnational Imaginary*, eds. Rob Wilson and Wimal Dissanayake. Durham and London: Duke University Press. 46–77.

Fentress, James, and Chris Wickham. 1992. *Social Memory.* Oxford, UK and Cambridge, MA: Blackwell.

Foucault, Michel. 1986. "Of Other Spaces." *Diacritics* 16: 22–27.

George, Rosemary Marangoly. 1996. *The Politics of Home: Postcolonial Relations and Twentieth-century Fiction.* Cambridge: Cambridge University Press.

Gill, Lakshmi. 1990. "Me." In *Shakti's Words: An Anthology of South Asian Canadian Women's Poetry*, eds. Diane McGifford and Judith Kearns. Toronto: TSAR. 30.

———.1990. "Immigrant Always." In *Shakti's Words: An Anthology of South Asian Canadian Women's Poetry*, eds. Diane McGifford and Judith Kearns. Toronto: TSAR. 33.

Gillis, John R. 1994. "Memory and Identity: The History of a Relationship." In *Commemorations: The Politics of National Identity*, ed. John R. Gillis. Princeton: Princeton University Press. 3–24.

Gordon, Avery. 1997. *Ghostly Matters: Haunting and the Sociological Imagination.* Minneapolis: University of Minnesota Press.

Goto, Edy. 1981. "The Dream." *West Coast Review* 16: 5–8.

Grossberg, Lawrence. 1996. "The Space of Culture, The Power of Space." In *The Post-Colonial Question: Common Skies, Divided Horizons*, eds. Iain Chambers and Lidia Curti. London and New York: Routledge. 169–188.

Gunn, Sean. 1979. "Orientation #1." In *Inalienable Rice: A Chinese and Japanese Canadian Anthology*, eds. Garrick Chu, et al. Vancouver: Powell Street Revue and the Chinese Canadian Writers' Workshop. 38.

Ha Jin. 1996. "In New York City." In *Facing Shadows*. Brooklyn, NY: Hanging Loose Press. 62.

———.1996. "The Past." In *Facing Shadows*. Brooklyn, NY: Hanging Loose Press. 63.

———.1996. "To Ah Shu." In *Facing Shadows*. Brooklyn, NY: Hanging Loose Press. 65–67.

———.1990. "To an Ancient Chinese Poet." In *Between Silences: A Voice from China*. Chicago: University of Chicago Press. 65–66.

Hagedorn, Jessica. 2002. "Autobiography Part One." In *Danger and Beauty*. San Francisco: City Lights. 7–8.

———.2002. "Souvenirs." In *Danger and Beauty*. San Francisco: City Lights. 26–29.

Hahn, Kimiko. 1992. "The Izu Dancer." In *Earshot*. Brooklyn, NY: Hanging Loose Press. 87–93.

Hall, Catherine. 1996. "Histories, Empires and the Post-colonial Moment." In *The Post-Colonial Question: Common Skies, Divided Horizon*, eds. Iain Chambers and Lidia Curti. London and New York: Routledge. 65–77.

Hall, Stuart. 1993. "For Allon White: Metaphors of Transformation." In *Carnival, Hysteria, and Writing: Collected Essays and Autobiography* (by Allon White). Oxford: Clarendon Press. 1–25.

———.1990. "Cultural Identity and Diaspora." In *Identity: Community, Culture, Difference*, ed. Jonathan Rutherford. London: Lawrence and Wishart. 222–237.

———.1989. "Ethnicity: Identity and Difference." *Radical America* 23: 9–20.

———.1987. "Minimal Selves." In *Identity: the Real Me*, ed. Lisa Appignanesi. ICA Documents No. 6, London: Institute of Contemporary Arts. 44–46.

Hawley, John C. 1996. "Introduction." In *Cross-Addressing: Resistance Literature and Cultural Borders*, ed. John C. Hawley. Albany, NY: State University of New York Press. 1–12.

Heidegger, Martin. 1993. *Basic Writings*, ed. David Farrell Krell. London and New York: Routledge.

Hejinian, Lyn. 2002. "Poetic Statement: Some Notes toward a Poetics." In *American Women Poets in the 21st Century: Where Lyric Meets Language*, eds. Claudia Rankine and Juliana Spahr. Middletown, CT: Wesleyan University Press. 235–241.

Heung, Marina. 1993. "Daughter-Text/Mother-Text: Matrilineage in Amy Tan's *Joy Luck Club*." *Feminist Studies* 19: 597–616.

Hirschkop, Ken. 1989. "Introduction: Bakhtin and Cultural Theory." In *Bakhtin and Cultural Theory*, eds. Ken Hirschkop and David Shepherd. Manchester: Manchester University Press. 1–38.

Holquist, J. Michael. 1985. "The Carnival of Discourse: Baxtin and Simultaneity." *Canadian Review of Comparative Literature* 12: 220–34.

Hom, Sharon K. 1999. "[Per]forming Law: Deformations and Transformations." In *Chinese Women Traversing Diaspora: Memoirs, Essays, and Poetry*, ed. Sharon K. Hom. New York and London: Garland. 127–144.

Hongo, Garrett. 1996. "O-Bon: Dance for the Dead." In *The River of Heaven*. New York: Alfred A. Knopf. 14–15.

———.1996. "The Legend." In *The River of Heaven*. New York: Alfred A. Knopf. 66–67.

hooks, bell. 1989. "Choosing the Margin as a Space of Radical Openness." *Framework* 36: 15–24.

Huang, Guiyou. 2002. "Introduction: The Makers of the Asian American Poetic Landscape." In *Asian American Poets: A Bio-bibliographical Critical Sourcebook*, ed. Guiyou Huang. Westport, CT and London: Greenwood Press. 1–14.

Inada, Lawson Fusao. 1997. "In a Buddhist Forest." In *Drawing the Line*. Minneapolis: Coffee House Press. 47.

———.1997. "Kicking the Habit." In *Drawing the Line*. Minneapolis: Coffee House Press. 48–51.

———.1993. "Memory." In *Legends from Camp*. Minneapolis: Coffee House Press. 50–51.

———.1993. "Headwaters." In *Legends from Camp*. Minneapolis: Coffee House Press. 160–165.

———.1993. "Red Earth, Blue Sky, Petrified." In *Legends from Camp*. Minneapolis: Coffee House Press. 176–177.

Irie, Kevin. 1996. "Flight: An Immigrant's Memory." In *Another Way to Dance: Contemporary Asian Poetry from Canada and the United States*, ed. Cyril Dabydeen. Toronto: TSAR. 88–89.

Iser, Wolfgang. 1996. "The Emergence of a Cross-Cultural Discourse: Thomas Carlyle's Sartor Resartus." In *The Translatability of Cultures: Figurations of the Space Between*, eds. Sanford Budick and Wolfgang Iser. Stanford: Stanford University Press. 245–264.

Ismail, Jam. 1991. "From Scared Texts." In *Many-Mouthed Birds: Contemporary Writing by Chinese Canadians*, eds. Bennett Lee and Jim Wong-Chu. Vancouver and Toronto: Douglas and McIntyre. 124–135.

Ito, Sally. 1996. "Sansei." In *Breathing Fire: Canada's New Poets*, eds. Lorna Crozier and Patrick Lane. Madeira Park, BC: Harbour Publishing. 91–92.

JanMohamed, Abdul R. 1992. "Worldliness-without-World, Homeless-ness-as-Home: Toward a Definition of the Specular Border Intellectual." In *Edward Said: A Critical Reader*, ed. Michael Sprinker. Oxford, UK and Cambridge, MA: Blackwell. 96–120.

JanMohamed, Abdul R. and David Lloyd. 1990. "Introduction: Toward a Theory of Minority Discourse: What is to be Done?" In *The Nature and Context of Minority Discourse*, eds. Abdul R. JanMohamed and David Lloyd. Oxford: Oxford University Press. 1–16.

Jay, Paul. 2001. "Beyond Discipline? Globalization and the Future of English." *PMLA* 116.1: 32–47.

Johnson, David E., and Scott Michaelsen. 1997. "Border Secrets: An Introduction." In *Border Theory: The Limits of Cultural Politics*, eds. David E. Johnson and Scott Michaelsen. Minneapolis: University of Minnesota Press. 1–42.

Jullien, François. 2000. *Detour and Access: Strategies of Meaning in China and Greece*, trans. Sophie Hawkes. New York: Zone Books.

———.1995. *The Propensity of Things toward a History of Efficacy in China*, trans. Janet Lloyd. New York: Zone Books.

Kalsey, Surjeet. 1990. "Breaking the Silence." In *Shakti's Words: An Anthology of South Asian Canadian Women's Poetry*, eds. Diane McGifford and Judith Kearns. Toronto: TSAR. 46–47.

———.1990. "Migratory Birds." In *Shakti's Words: An Anthology of South Asian Canadian Women's Poetry*, eds. Diane McGifford and Judith Kearns. Toronto: TSAR. 40.

Kaplan, David H. 1999. "Territorial Identities and Geographic Scale." In *Nested Identities: Nationalism, Territory, and Scale*, eds. Guntram H. Herb and David. H. Kaplan. Lanham, MD: Rowman and Littlefield Publishers. 31–52.

Kim, Elaine H. 1982. *Asian American Literature: An Introduction to the Writings and their Social Context*. Philadelphia: Temple University Press.

Kim, Myung Mi. 1995. "Anna O Addendum." In *Premonitions: The Kaya Anthology of New Asian North American Poetry*, ed. Walter K. Lew. New York: Kaya Production. 360–370.

Kiyooka, Roy. 1981. "Dear M." *West Coast Review* 16: 18.

Kogawa, Joy. 1985. "She is not a Fence Sitter." In *Woman in the Woods*. Oakville, NY and London: Mosaic Press. 33.

———.1985. "For Ben and Malcolm." In *Woman in the Woods*. Oakville, NY and London: Mosaic Press. 58.

———.1985. "Minerals from Stone." In *Woman in the Woods*. Oakville, NY and London: Mosaic Press. 64.

———.1977. "Once When We Were Rejected." In *Jericho Road*. Toronto: McClelland and Stewart. 56.

———.1974. "This is a Clearing." In *A Choice of Dream*. Toronto: McClelland and Stewart. 18.

Kristeva, Julia. 1991. *Strangers to Ourselves*, trans. Leon S. Roudiez. New York: Columbia University Press.

———.1980a. *Desire in Language: A Semiotic Approach to Literature and Art*, trans. Thomas Gora, Alice Jardine and Leon S. Roudiez. New York: Columbia University Press.

———.1980b. "Postmodernism." In *Romanticism, Modernism, Postmodernism*, ed. Harry R. Garvin. Lewisburg, PA: Bucknell University Press. 136–141.

Kwa, Lydia. 1994. "Travelling Time." In *The Colours of Heroins*. Toronto: Women's Press. 26–29.

Laiwan. 1991. "The Imperialism of Syntax." In *Many-Mouthed Birds: Contemporary Writing by Chinese Canadians*, eds. Bennett Lee and Jim Wong-Chu. Vancouver and Toronto: Douglas and McIntyre. 57–58.

Lambek, Michael. 2003. "Memory in a Maussian Universe." In *Regimes of Memory*, eds. Susannah Radstone and Katharine Hodgkin. London and New York: Routledge. 202–216.

Langworthy, Christian. 2000. "How I Could Interpret the Events of my Youth, Events I do not Remember except in Dreams." In *Asian American Literature: An Anthology*, ed. Shirley Geok-Lin Lim. Lincolnwood, IL: NTC Publishing Group. 60–61.

Lau, Evelyn. 1994. "The Monks' Song." In *In the House of Slaves*. Toronto: Coach House Press. 44.

Lavie, Smadar, and Ted Swedenburg. 1996. "Introduction." In *Displacement, Diaspora, and Geographies of Identity*, eds. Smadar Lavie and Ted Swedenburg. Durham and London: Duke University Press. 1–26.

Lee, Leo Ou-fan. 1994. "On the Margins of Chinese Discourse: Some Personal Thoughts on the Cultural Meaning of the Periphery." In *The Living Tree: The Changing Meaning of Being Chinese Today*, ed. Wei-ming Tu. Stanford: Stanford University Press. 221–244.

Lee, Li-Young. 2001. "Discrepancies, Happy and Sad." In *Book of My Nights*. Rochester, NY: BOA Editions. 22.

———.2001. "Restless." In *Book of My Nights*. Rochester, NY: BOA Editions. 58–60.

———.2000. "Li-Young Lee: Interview by James Kyung-Jin Lee." In *Words Matter: Conversations with Asian American Writers*, ed. King-kok Cheung. Honolulu, HI: University of Hawai'i Press. 270–282.

———.1990. "Furious Versions." In *The City in Which I Love You*. Rochester, NY: BOA Editions. 13–29.

———.1986. "The Gift." In *Rose: Poems by Li-Young Lee*. Rochester, NY: BOA Editions. 15–16.

———.1986. "Mnemonic." In *Rose: Poems by Li-Young Lee*. Rochester, NY: BOA Editions. 66.

Lee, Pwu Jean. 1997. "A Guitar." In *East Wind, West Rain: Poems*. Lewiston, NY: The Edwin Mellen Press. 13.

Lefebvre, Henri. 1991. *The Production of Space*, trans. Donald Nicholson-Smith. Oxford, UK and Cambridge, MA: Blackwell.

Leong, Russell. 2000. "Russell Leong: Interview by Robert B. Ito." In *Words Matter: Conversations with Asian American Writers*, ed. King-kok Cheung. Honolulu, HI: University of Hawai'i Press. 233–251.

———.1993. "Aerogrammes." In *The Country of Dreams and Dust*. Albuquerque, NM: West End Press. 5–15.

———.1993. "Flume." In *The Country of Dreams and Dust*. Albuquerque, NM: West End Press. 47–49.

Leung, Ho Hon. 1995. "A Symphonic Poem 'Unfinished.'" In *Premonitions: The Kaya Anthology of New Asian North American Poetry*, ed. Walter K. Lew. New York: Kaya Production. 247–248.

Lim, Shirley Geok-lin. 1998. "Father in China." In *What the Fortune Teller Didn't Say*. Albuquerque, MN: West End Press. 19–20.

———.1997. "Immigration and Diaspora." In *An Interethnic Companion to Asian American Literature*, ed. King-kok Cheung. Cambridge: Cambridge University Press. 289–311.

———.1994. "I Remember." In *Monsoon History: Selected Poems*. London: Skoob Books. 35.

———.1994. "To What Ends." In *Monsoon History: Selected Poems*. London: Skoob Books. 76.

———.1994. "An Immigrant Looks at Whitman." In *Monsoon History: Selected Poems*. London: Skoob Books. 91.

———.1994. "I Defy You." In *Monsoon History: Selected Poems*. London: Skoob Books. 93.

———.1993. "Assaying the Gold: or: Contesting the Ground of Asian American." *New Literary History* 24: 147–69.

Lim, Shirley Geok-lin, Larry E. Smith, and Wimal Dissanayake, eds. 1999. *Transnational Asian Pacific: Gender, Culture, and the Public Sphere*. Urbana: University of Illinois Press.

Liu, Stephen. 1981. "My Father's Martial Art." *The Antioch Review* 39.3: 82–83.

Liu, Timothy. 1992. "Awaiting Translation." In *Vox Angelica: Poems by Timothy Liu*. Cambridge, MA: Alice James Books. 12.

Lovell, Nadia. 1998. "Introduction: Belonging in Need of Emplacement." In *Locality and Belonging*, ed. Nadia Lovell. London and New York: Routledge. 1–13.

Lowe, Lisa. 1991: "Heterogeneity, Hybridity, Multiplicity: Making Asian American Differences." *Diaspora* 1: 24–44.

Lum, Wing Tek. 1991. "Chinese Hot Pot." In *Chinese American Poetry: An Anthology*, eds. L. Ling-chi Wang and Henry Yiheng Zhao. Santa Barbara, CA: Asian American Voices. 163.

———.1991. "T-Bone Steak." In *Chinese American Poetry: An Anthology*, eds. L. Ling-chi Wang and Henry Yiheng Zhao. Santa Barbara, CA: Asian American Voices. 167–168.

Manan. 1997. "Unfettered at last, a traveling monk." In *The Penguin Book of Zen Poetry*, eds. and trans. Lucien Stryk and Takashi Ikemoto. London: Allen Lane. 76.

Mark, Diane Mei Lin. 1991. "Suzie Wong Doesn't Live Here." In *Chinese American Poetry: An Anthology*, eds. L. Ling-chi Wang and Henry Yiheng Zhao. Santa Barbara, CA: Asian American Voices. 182.

Massey, Doreen. 1994. *Space, Place and Gender*. Oxford: Polity Press.

———.1993. "Power-geometry and a Progressive Sense of Place." In *Mapping the Futures: Local Cultures, Global Change*, eds. Jon Bird, et al. London and New York: Routledge. 59–69.

Metz, Christian. 1982. *The Imaginary Signifier: Psychoanalysis and the Cinema*, trans. Celia Britton, Annwyl Williams, Ben Brewster and Alfred Guzzetti. Bloomington: Indiana University Press.

Miki, Roy. 1995. "From *Market Rinse*." In *Premonitions: The Kaya Anthology of New Asian North American Poetry*, ed. Walter K. Lew. New York: Kaya Production. 283–286.

Mills, Charles W. 1997. *The Racial Contract*. Ithaca and London: Cornell University Press.

Minh-ha, Trinh T. 1989. *Woman, Native, Other*. Bloomington: Indiana University Press.

Mitchell, Katharyne. 1997. "Transnational Subjects: Constituting the Cultural Citizen in the Era of Pacific Rim Capital." In *Ungrounded Empires: The Cultural Politics of Modern Chinese Transnationalism*, eds. Aihwa Ong and Donald M. Nonini. New York and London: Routledge. 228–260.

Mohanty, Chandra Talpade. 1991. "Introduction: Cartographies of Struggle: Third World Women and the Politics of Feminism." In *Third World Women and the Politics of Feminism*, eds. Chandra Talpade Mohanty, Ann Russo and Lourdes Torres. Bloomington: Indiana University Press. 1–47.

Mura, David. 1995. "Issei: Song of the First Years in America." In *The Colors of Desire*. New York and London: Anchor. 15–17.

Naficy, Hamid. 1996. "Phobic Spaces and Liminal Panics: Independent Transnational Film Centre." In *Global/Local: Cultural Production and the Transnational Imaginary*, eds. Rob Wilson and Wimal Dissanayake. Durham and London: Duke University Press. 119–144.

Needham, Lawrence. 1995. "'Goody Two-shoes'/'Goosee Shoo-shoo': Translated Tales of Resistance in Matthew Lewis's *Journal of a West India Proprietor*." In *Between Languages and Cultures: Translation and Cross-Cultural Texts*, eds. Anuradha Dingwaney and Carol Maier. Pittsburgh and London: University of Pittsburgh Press. 103–118.

Ng, Franklin. 1998. "Volume Introduction." In *Adaptation, Acculturation, and Transnational Ties among Asian Americans*, ed. Franklin Ng. New York and London: Garland. ix-xi.

Ng, Lucy. 1991. "The Sullen Shapes of Poems." In *Many-Mouthed Birds: Contemporary Writing by Chinese Canadians*, eds. Bennett Lee and Jim Wong-Chu. Vancouver and Toronto: Douglas and McIntyre. 160–168.

Nora, Pierre. 1996. "Introduction to *Realms of Memory, Volume II*." In *Realms of Memory, Volume II*, ed. Lawrence D. Kritzman, and trans. Arthur Goldhammer. New York: Columbia University Press. ix-xii.

———.1989. "Between Memory and History: *Les lieux de mémoire.*" *Representations* 26: 7–25.

Novick, Peter. 1988. *That Noble Dream: The "Objective Question" and the American Historical Profession.* Cambridge: Cambridge University Press.

———.1999. *The Holocaust in American Life.* Boston: Houghton Mifflin Campany.

Nygren, Scott. 1993. "Doubleness and Idiosyncrasy in Cross-Cultural Analysis." In *Otherness and the Media: The Ethnography of the Imagined and the Imaged,* eds. Namid Naficy and Teshome H. Gabriel. Langhorne, PA: Harwood Academic Publishers. 173–187.

Okano, Haruko. 1992. *Come Spring.* North Vancouver: Gallerie.

Ong, Aihwa. 1999. *Flexible Citizenship: The Cultural Logics of Transnationality.* Durham and London: Duke University Press.

Palumbo-Liu, David. 1999. *Asian/American: Historical Crossings of a Racial Frontier.* Stanford: Stanford University Press.

Papastergiadis, Nikos. 1998. *Dialogues in the Diasporas: Essays and Conversations on Cultural Identity.* London: Rivers Oram.

Parameswaran, Uma. 1990. "Sharad" In *Another Way to Dance: Asian Canadian Poetry,* ed. Cyril Dabydeen. Stratford, ON: Williams-Wallace. 88.

Peeradina, Saleem. 1995. "Reflections on the Other." In *Living in America: Poetry and Fiction by South Asian American Writers,* ed. Roshni Rustomji-Kerns. Boulder, San Francisco and Oxford: Westview Press. 59–61.

Pratt, Mary Louise. 1995. "Comparative Literature and Global Citizenship." In *Comparative Literature in the Age of Multiculturalism,* ed. Charles Bernheimer. Baltimore and London: The Johns Hopkins University Press. 58–65.

———.1992. *Imperial Eyes: Travel Writing and Transculturation.* London and New York: Routledge.

Radhakrishnan, R. 1996. *Diasporic Mediations: Between Home and Location.* Minneapolis: University of Minnesota Press.

Rajan, Tilottama. 1990. "Victims of the War." In *Shakti's Words: An Anthology of South Asian Canadian Women's Poetry,* eds. Diane McGifford and Judith Kearns. Toronto: TSAR. 86–87.

Raymond, Janice. 1986. *A Passion for Friends: Toward a Philosophy of Female Affection.* London: Women's Press.

Rushdie, Salman. 1991. *Imaginary Homelands: Essays and Criticism 1981–1991.* London: Granta.

Said, Edward. 1984a. "The Mind of Winter: Reflections on Life in Exile." *Harper's Magazine* 269: 49–55.

———. 1984b. "Reflections on Exile." *Granta* 13: 159–172.

———. 1979. *Orientalism.* New York: Vintage.

Saijo, Albert. 1997. *Outspeaks: A Rhapsody.* Honolulu, HI: Bamboo Ridge Press.

Seto, Thelma. 1995. “Living in the Margins.” In *Premonitions: The Kaya Anthology of New Asian North American Poetry*, ed. Walter K. Lew. New York: Kaya Production. 161–165.

Shohat, Ella, and Robert Stam. 1994. *Unthinking Eurocentrism: Multiculturalism and the Media.* London and New York: Routledge.

Song, Cathy. 1988. “Heaven.” In *Frameless Windows, Squares of Lights*. New York and London: W. W. Norton. 77–79.

———.1983. “Beauty and Sadness.” In *Picture Bride*. New Haven: Yale University Press. 37.

Soo, Ben. 1991. “Prentiss and the Island.” In *Many-Mouthed Birds: Contemporary Writing by Chinese Canadians*, eds. Bennett Lee and Jim Wong-Chu. Vancouver and Toronto: Douglas and McIntyre. 93–104.

Spivak, Gayatri C. 1990. “Poststructuralism, Marginality, Postcoloniality and Value.” In *Literary Theory Toda,* eds. Peter Collier and Helga Geyer-Ryan. Cambridge: Polity Press. 219–244.

Sponsler, Claire. 2000. “Introduction.” In *East of West: Cross-Cultural Performance and the Staging of Difference*, eds. Claire Sponsler and Xiaomei Chen. New York: Palgrave. 1–14.

Stallybrass, Peter. 1989. “Drunk with the Cup of Liberty.” In *The Violence of Representation: Literature and the History of Violence*, eds. Nancy Armstrong and Leonard Tennenhouse. London and New York: Routledge. 45–76.

Sumida, Stephen H. 2000. “The More Things Change: Paradigm Shifts in Asian American Studies.” *American Studies International* 38: 97–114.

Sze, Arthur. 1999. “Response.” In *Yellow Light: The Flowering of Asian American Arts*, ed. Amy Ling. Philadelphia: Temple University Press. 74–76.

———.1998. “The Network.” In *The Redshifting Web*, Port Townsend, WA: Copper Canyon Press. 122.

———.1998. “Every Where and Every When.” In *The Redshifting Web*, Port Townsend, WA: Copper Canyon Press. 139–141.

———.1995. “Archipelago.” In *Archipelago*. Port Townsend, WA: Copper Canyon Press. 75–81.

Tabios, Eileen, ed. 1998. *Black Lightning: Poetry-in-progress*. New York: Asian American Writers’ Workshop.

Terdiman, Richard. 2003. “Given Memory: On Mnemonic Coercion, Reproduction, and Invention.” In *Regimes of Memory*, eds. Susannah Radstone and Katharine Hodgkin. London and New York: Routledge. 186–201.

Thúy, Lê Thi Diem. 2000. “Shrapnel Shards on Blue Water.” In *Asian American Literature: An Anthology*, ed. Shirley Geok-Lin Lim. Lincolnwood, IL: NTC Publishing Group. 224–226.

Trang, Jora. 2000. “Legacy.” In *Tilting the Continent: Southeast Asian American Writing*, eds. Shirley Geok-lin Lim and Cheng Lok Chua. Minneapolis: New Rivers Press. 30–32.

Tu, Wei-ming, ed. 1994. *The Living Tree: The Changing Meaning of Being Chinese Today*. Stanford: Stanford University Press.

TuSmith, Bonnie. 1993. *All My Relatives: Community in Contemporary Ethnic American Literatures*. Ann Arbor: University of Michigan Press.

Vasudeva, Amita. 1995. "Can you Talk Mexican?" In *Living in America: Poetry and Fiction by South Asian American Writers*, ed. Roshni Rustomji-Kerns. Boulder, San Francisco and Oxford: Westview Press. 70–71.

Venuti, Lawrence. 1995. *The Translator's Invisibility: A History of Translation*. London and New York: Routledge.

Villa, José Garcia. 1988. *55 Poems Selected and Translated into Tagalog*, trans. Hilario S. Francia. Quezon City: University of the Philippines Press.

———.1962. "Definitions of Poetry." In *Filipino Essays in English 1910–1954*, Vol. 1, ed. Leopoldo Y. Yabes. Quezon City: University of the Philippines Press.

Voris, Linda. 2002. "A 'Sensitive Empiricism': Berssenbrugge's Phenomenological Investigations." In *American Women Poets in the 21st Century: Where Lyric Meets Language*, eds. Claudia Rankine and Juliana Spahr. Middletown, CT: Wesleyan University Press. 68–17.

Vuong-Riddick, Thuong. 1995. "Searching." In *Two Shores/Deux Rives: Poems/Poèmes*. Vancouver: Ronsdale Press. 1.

———.1995. "Day and Night." In *Two Shores/Deux Rives: Poems/Poèmes*. Vancouver: Ronsdale Press. 70–71.

———.1995. "For My Father." In *Two Shores/Deux Rives: Poems/Poèmes*. Vancouver: Ronsdale Press. 114–117.

Wah, Fred. 1991. "Elite." In *Many-Mouthed Birds: Contemporary Writing by Chinese Canadians*, eds. Bennett Lee and Jim Wong-Chu. Vancouver and Toronto: Douglas and McIntyre. 169–179.

———.1981. "mmmmmm." In *Breathin' My Name with a Sigh*. Vancouver: Talonbooks. 9.

———.1981. "WHAT'S IT LIKE TO HOLD YOURSELF IN." In *Breathin' My Name with a Sigh*. Vancouver: Talonbooks. 39.

———.1981. "WANT RIVER PIECE OUT OF THIS MOVING RIVER." In *Breathin' My Name with a Sigh*. Vancouver: Talonbooks. 40.

———.1980. "Pictograms from the Interior of B.C." In *Selected Poems: Loki is Buried at Smoky Creek*, ed. George Bowering. Vancouver: Talonbooks. 91–96.

West, William N. 2003. "'No Endless Moniment': Artificial Memory and Memorial Artifact in Early Modern England." In *Regimes of Memory*, eds. Susannah Radstone and Katharine Hodgkin. London and New York: Routledge. 61–75.

White, Allon. 1993. *Carnival, Hysteria, and Writing: Collected Essays and Autobiography*. Oxford: Clarendon Press.

Wilson, Rob, and Wimal Dissanayake. 1996. "Introduction: Tracking the Global/Local." In *Global/Local: Cultural Production and the Transnational Imaginary*, eds. Rob Wilson and Wimal Dissanayake. Durham and London: Duke University Press. 1–20.

Wong, Nellie. 2003. "It's in the Blood." In *From Totems to Hip-Hop: A Multicultural Anthology of Poetry Across the Americas, 1990–2002*, ed. Ishmael Reed. New York: Thunder's Mouth Press. 183–186.

Wong, Rita. 1999. "grammar poem." In *Swallowing Clouds: An Anthology of Chinese-Canadian Poetry*, eds. Andy Quan and Jim Wong-Chu. Vancouver: Pulp Press. 23.

Wong, Sau-ling Cynthia. 1995. "Denationalization Reconsidered: Asian American Cultural Criticism at a Theoretical Crossroads," *Amerasia Journal* 21: 1–27.

———.1993. *Reading Asian American Literature: From Necessity to Extravagance*. Princeton: Princeton University Press.

Wong, Sunn Shelley. 2001. "Sizing Up Asian American Poetry." In *A Resource Guide to Asian American Literature*, eds. Sau-ling Cynthia Wong and Stephen H. Sumida. New York: MLA. 285–308.

Wong-Chu, Jim. 1996. "Peasants." In *Another Way to Dance: Contemporary Asian Poetry from Canada and the United States*, ed. Cyril Dabydeen. Toronto: TSAR. 234.

———.1996. "Fourth Uncle." In *Another Way to Dance: Contemporary Asian Poetry from Canada and the United States*, ed. Cyril Dabydeen. Toronto: TSAR. 235.

———.1996. "Old Chinese Cemetery: Kamloops July 1977." In *Another Way to Dance: Contemporary Asian Poetry from Canada and the United States*, ed. Cyril Dabydeen. Toronto: TSAR. 237.

———.1991. "How Feel I Do?" In *Many-Mouthed Birds: Contemporary Writing by Chinese Canadians*, eds. Bennett Lee and Jim Wong-Chu. Vancouver and Toronto: Douglas and McIntyre. 17.

———.1986. "Tradition." In *Chinatown Ghosts*, Vancouver: Pulp Press. 11.

Woo, David. 1993. "Habit." In *The Open Boat: Poems from Asian America*, ed. Garrett Hongo. New York: Anchor. 287.

Woo, Merle. 1991. "Yellow Woman Speaks." In *Chinese American Poetry: An Anthology*, eds. L. Ling-chi Wang and Henry Yiheng Zhao. Santa Barbara, CA: Asian American Voices. 216.

Yamada, Mitsuye. 1998. "Block 4 Barrack 4 'Apt' C." In *Camp Notes and Other Writings*. New Brunswick, NJ: Rutgers University Press. 19.

———.1988. "Desert Run." In *Desert Run*. Latham, NY: Kitchen Table: Women of Color Press. 1–5.

———.1988. "Masks of Woman." In *Desert Run*. Latham, NY: Kitchen Table: Women of Color Press. 87–89.

Yau, John. 2002. "830 Fireplace Road." In *Borrowed Love Poems*. New York: Penguin. 12.

———.1996. "Genghis Chan: Private Eye XXV." In *Forbidden Entries*. Santa Rosa: Black Sparrow Press. 103.

———.1996. "Genghis Chan: Private Eye XXVII." In *Forbidden Entries*. Santa Rosa: Black Sparrow Press. 105.

———.1992. "Postcard 16." In *Edificio Sayonara.* Santa Rosa: Black Sparrow Press. 108–109.

Yuan, Yuan. 1999. "The Semiotics of China Narratives in the Con/texts of Kingston and Tan." *Critique* 40: 292–303.

Yung, Eleanor S. 1999. "Moving into Stillness." In *Chinese Women Traversing Diaspora: Memoirs, Essays, and Poetry*, ed. Sharon K. Hom. New York and London: Garland. 165–187.

Zarco, Cyn. 1995. "Magdalena's Vision." In *Premonitions: The Kaya Anthology of New Asian North American Poetry*, ed. Walter K. Lew. New York: Kaya Production. 130.

Zavala, Iris M. 1988. "Bakhtin Versus the Postmodern." *Sociocriticism* 4: 51–69.

Zhang, Benzi. 1996. "Japanese-American Literature." In *New Immigrant Literatures in the United States: A Sourcebook to Our Multicultural Literary Heritage*, ed. Alpana S. Knippling. Westport, CT and London: Greenwood Press. 125–141.

Zhang, Longxi. 1998. *Mighty Opposites: From Dichotomies to Differences in the Comparative Study of China.* Stanford: Stanford University Press.

Zhang, Zhen. 1999. "Deep into Småland." In *Chinese Women Traversing Diaspora: Memoirs, Essays, and Poetry*, ed. Sharon K. Hom. New York and London: Garland. 101–102.

Index

Y

Z

For Product Safety Concerns and Information please contact our EU representative GPSR@taylorandfrancis.com
Taylor & Francis Verlag GmbH, Kaufingerstraße 24, 80331 München, Germany

www.ingramcontent.com/pod-product-compliance
Lightning Source LLC
Chambersburg PA
CBHW071435100726
47908CB00004B/1164

* 9 7 8 0 4 1 5 5 1 2 8 6 2 *